W0461423

shooter

shooter

stimulating shots with a kick

Parragon

Bath · New York · Singapore · Hong Kong · Cologne · Delhi · Melbourne

First published by Parragon in 2007

Parragon
Queen Street House
4 Queen Street
Bath BA1 1HE

Copyright © Parragon Books Ltd 2007

Designed by Talking Design
Photography by Mike Cooper
Introduction text and additional recipes by Linda Doeser
Food Styling by Lincoln Jefferson and Carole Handslip

All rights reserved. No part of this publication may be reproduced, stored in a retrieval system, or transmitted in any way or by any means, electronic, mechanical, photocopying, recording or otherwise, without the prior permission of the copyright holder.

ISBN 978-1-4054-9508-0

Printed in China

WARNING

Recipes containing raw eggs are not suitable for convalescents, the elderly or pregnant women. Please consume alcohol responsibly.

CONTENTS

introduction

Often colourful, invariably tasty and with truly bizarre names, shooters are terrifically popular. Several servings can be made simultaneously as they are always served in small glasses. Making shooters isn't difficult and is great fun. Reading the following basic guidelines should ensure you have all the skills of a professional bartender at your fingertips.

Measures

Measuring the quantities is one of the keys to making a good cocktail. The standard single measure is 25 ml/1 fl oz, as used throughout this book. You can decide to use your own standard measure as long as you follow the proportions given in the recipes.

Bar Essentials

Cocktail shaker The standard type is a cylindrical 500-ml/18-fl oz container with a double lid incorporating a strainer. The Boston shaker consists of double conical containers without a strainer.

Mixing glass You can use the container of your cocktail shaker, a jug about the same size or a professional mixing glass.

Strainer A bar strainer prevents ice from being poured into the serving glass. You could also use a small nylon sieve.

Jigger This small measuring cup is often double-ended. Standard jiggers are 25 ml/1 fl oz and 35 ml/1½ fl oz, representing 1 and 1½ measures respectively. If you don't have a jigger, use a liqueur, schnapps or shot glass.

Bar spoon This long-handled spoon is used for stirring cocktails in a mixing glass.

Other basics Lots of ordinary kitchen equipment is useful: corkscrew, citrus juicer, chopping

board and kitchen knives. You will require an ice bucket and tongs.

Glasses

Cocktail glass Stemmed glass with a cone-shaped bowl (125–150 ml/4–5 fl oz)

Parfait glass Short-stemmed tube-shaped glass (25–50 ml/1–2 fl oz)

Pousse-café glass Short-stemmed tulip-shaped glass (50 ml/2 fl oz)

Shot glass Small glass (50 ml/2 fl oz)

Bartender's Tips

Shaking cocktails Remove the lid from the shaker, add ice and pour in the ingredients. Close and shake vigorously for 10–20 seconds, until the outside of the shaker is misty. Remove the small lid and pour the cocktail into the glass. If your shaker doesn't have an integral strainer, use a separate one.

Stirring cocktails Put ice into a mixing glass, pour in the ingredients and stir vigorously for 20 seconds. Strain into a glass.

Layering pousse-café To make a multi-layered drink, slowly pour the liqueurs or spirits over the back of a teaspoon into the glass. Each layer then settles on top of the layer before it.

Ice To crack ice, put cubes in a strong plastic bag and hit with the smooth side of a meat mallet or a rolling pin. Alternatively, bang the bag against a wall.

Chilling glasses Place glasses in the refrigerator for 2 hours before using. Alternatively, fill them with cracked ice, stir well, then tip out the ice before pouring in the cocktail.

Party Starter

Tequila Slammer

SLAMMERS ARE A TYPE OF SHOOTER. THE IDEA IS THAT YOU POUR THE INGREDIENTS DIRECTLY INTO THE GLASS, WITHOUT STIRRING. COVER THE GLASS WITH ONE HAND TO PREVENT SPILLAGE, SLAM IT ON TO A TABLE TO MIX AND DRINK THE COCKTAIL DOWN IN ONE! DO ENSURE YOU USE A STRONG GLASS!

SERVES 1

1 measure white tequila, chilled
1 measure lemon juice
sparkling wine, chilled

1. Put the tequila and lemon juice into a chilled glass.
2. Top up with sparkling wine.
3. Cover the glass with your hand and slam.

Alabama Slammer

SMALL, BUT PERFECTLY PROPORTIONED – THIS IS A SHOOTER WITH A REAL KICK!

SERVES 1

1 measure Southern Comfort
1 measure Amaretto
½ measure sloe gin
½ tsp lemon juice

1. Pour the Southern Comfort, Amaretto and sloe gin over cracked ice in a mixing glass and stir.
2. Strain into a shot glass and add ½ tsp lemon juice.
3. Cover and slam.

Brain Haemorrhage

THIS IS A RARE INSTANCE OF A COCKTAIL THAT IS DELIBERATELY INTENDED TO LOOK HORRID, RATHER THAN TEMPTING, AND WAS PROBABLY INVENTED TO DRINK ON HALLOWEEN.

SERVES 1

1 measure chilled peach schnapps
1 tsp chilled Baileys Irish Cream
½ tsp chilled grenadine

1 Pour the peach schnapps into a shot glass, then carefully float the Baileys on top. Finally, top with the grenadine.

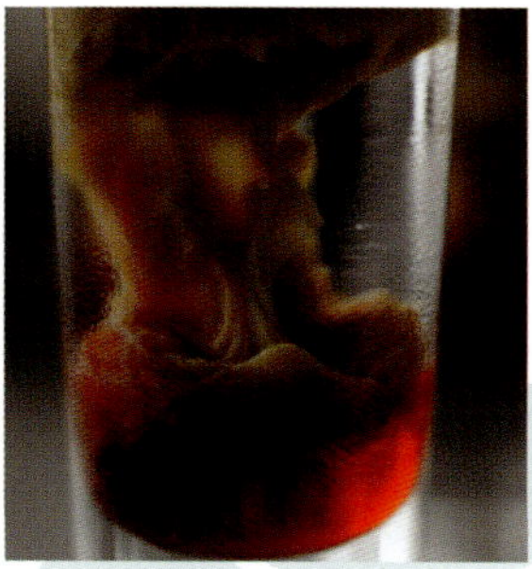

Firelighter

IF YOU ARE LOOKING FOR A COCKTAIL TO GIVE YOU A REAL KICK, THIS IS IT. THE INFAMOUS ABSINTHE IS A SERIOUSLY STRONG SPIRIT AND NOT TO BE TREATED LIGHTLY!

SERVES 1

1 measure absinthe, iced
1 measure lime juice cordial, iced

1 Ice a shot glass.
2 Shake the absinthe and lime over ice and, when well frosted, strain into the shot glass.

High Flyer

THESE TWO UNUSUAL LIQUEURS GIVE A VERY AROMATIC AND FRUITY COCKTAIL.

SERVES 1
⅔ measure gin
½ measure Strega
½ measure Van der Hum or Triple Sec
ice
orange or lemon peel, to decorate

1 Stir the first three ingredients well over ice and strain into a tumbler.
2 Finish with a twist of peel.

Tornado

IF THESE LIQUORS ARE REALLY WELL ICED, YOU WILL CERTAINLY CREATE A TORNADO IN YOUR GLASS WHEN YOU POUR ONE INTO THE OTHER – JUST SIT AND WATCH THEM SWIRLING FOR A MOMENT!

SERVES 1

1 measure peach or other favourite schnapps, frozen

1 measure black Sambuca, frozen

1. Pour the schnapps into an iced shot glass.
2. Then gently pour on the Sambuca over the back of a spoon.
3. Leave it for a few minutes to settle and separate before you down it.

Toffee Split

YOU SHOULD NOT NEED A DESSERT AS WELL, BUT YOU COULD ALWAYS POUR IT OVER SOME ICE CREAM.

SERVES 1

crushed ice

1 measure toffee liqueur, iced

2 measures Drambuie

1. Fill a small cocktail glass or shot glass with crushed ice.
2. Pour on the Drambuie and pour in the toffee liqueur carefully from the side of the glass so it layers on top.
3. Drink immediately.

White Diamond Frappé

THIS IS A CRAZY COMBINATION OF LIQUEURS, BUT IT WORKS WELL ONCE YOU'VE ADDED THE LEMON. EXTRA CRUSHED ICE AT THE LAST MINUTE BRINGS OUT ALL THE SEPARATE FLAVOURS.

SERVES 1

¼ measure peppermint schnapps
¼ measure white crème de cacao
¼ measure anise liqueur
¼ measure lemon juice
ice and crushed ice

1 Shake all the liquid ingredients over ice until frosted.
2 Strain into a chilled shot glass and add a small spoonful of crushed ice.

XYZ

ICE COOL, THIS BEAUTIFULLY SIMPLE COCKTAIL IS VERY REFRESHING AND MOREISH.

SERVES 1

½ measure fresh lemon juice
½ measure white rum
½ measure Cointreau
cracked ice
slice or twist of lime, to decorate

1 Shake all the liquid ingredients together over ice until well frosted.
2 Strain into a chilled glass and dress with a slice or twist of lime.

Aurora Borealis

THIS SPECTACULAR, COLOURED DRINK SHOULD NOT BE MIXED OR STIRRED. LEAVE IT TO SWIRL AROUND THE GLASS, CREATING A MULTI-HUED EFFECT AND TRY TO GUESS THE VARIOUS FLAVOURS.

SERVES 1

1 measure iced grappa or vodka
1 measure iced green Chartreuse
½ measure iced orange Curaçao
few drops iced cassis

1. Pour the grappa slowly round one side of a well-chilled shot glass.
2. Gently pour the Chartreuse round the other side.
3. Pour the Curaçao gently into the middle and add a few drops of cassis just before serving. Don't stir. Drink slowly!

Cowboy

IN MOVIES, COWBOYS DRINK THEIR RYE STRAIGHT, OFTEN PULLING THE CORK OUT OF THE BOTTLE WITH THEIR TEETH, AND IT IS CERTAINLY DIFFICULT TO IMAGINE JOHN WAYNE OR CLINT EASTWOOD SIPPING DELICATELY FROM A CHILLED COCKTAIL GLASS.

SERVES 1

3 measures rye whisky
2 tbsp single cream
cracked ice cubes

1 Pour the whisky and cream over ice and shake vigorously until well frosted.
2 Strain into a chilled glass.

Paradise

THIS FRUITY COMBINATION IS TRULY HEAVENLY WITH JUST A HINT OF SHARPNESS TO PREVENT IT FROM BECOMING SICKLY SWEET.

SERVES 1
cracked ice
1 measure gin
½ measure apricot brandy
½ measure freshly squeezed orange juice
dash of lemon juice

1. Put the ice in a cocktail shaker and pour in the gin, apricot brandy, orange juice and lemon juice.
2. Close the shaker and shake vigorously for 10–20 seconds, until the outside of the shaker is misted.
3. Strain into a glass.

Sangrita

AS YOU NEED TO MIX THE INGREDIENTS AT LEAST AN HOUR IN ADVANCE, THIS IS THE PERFECT DRINK TO SERVE TO GUESTS AND CLOSE FRIENDS.

SERVES 16

600 ml/1 pint tomato juice
300 ml/10 fl oz freshly squeezed orange juice
125 ml/4 fl oz freshly squeezed lime juice
1 jalapeño chilli, deseeded and finely chopped
1 tbsp Worcestershire sauce
1 tbsp Tabasco sauce
celery salt and ground white pepper
1 bottle (750 ml/26 fl oz) tequila, chilled

1. Pour the tomato juice, orange juice and lime juice into a large jug and stir in the chilli, Worcestershire sauce and Tabasco sauce. Season with celery salt and white pepper, then chill in the refrigerator for at least 1 hour, or longer if you want the mixture to taste spicier.
2. To serve, pour a measure of tequila into a shot glass and a measure of sangrita into a second shot glass. Drink the tequila in a single swallow, then chase with the sangrita.

Capucine

WELL-ICED LIQUEURS ARE OFTEN SERVED OVER FINELY CRUSHED ICE AS A FRAPPÉ. THIS VERSION IS TIERED FOR TWICE THE EFFECT.

SERVES 1
crushed ice
1 measure iced blue Curaçao
1 measure iced Parfait Amour

1. Pack a small cocktail or shot glass with finely crushed ice.
2. Pour in the Curaçao slowly and then carefully top up with the Parfait Amour.

Dandy

THE FRUIT FLAVOUR ADDED AT THE END IS WHAT GIVES THIS RICH COMBINATION A SPECIAL TOUCH.

SERVES 1

½ measure rye whisky
½ measure Dubonnet
dash of Angostura bitters
3 dashes cassis
ice
few frozen berries, to decorate

1. Mix the first four ingredients with ice and strain into an iced shot glass.
2. Dress with a berry or two.

Layered Lift-Off

Pousse-Café

A POUSSE-CAFÉ IS A LAYERED COCKTAIL OF MANY DIFFERENT COLOURED LIQUEURS. IT IS CRUCIAL TO ICE ALL THE LIQUEURS FIRST.

SERVES 1

¼ measure grenadine
¼ measure crème de menthe
¼ measure Galliano
¼ measure kümmel
¼ measure brandy

1 Ice all the liqueurs and a tall shot or pousse-café glass.
2 Carefully pour the liqueurs over a spoon evenly into the glass.
3 Leave for a few minutes to settle.

Angel's Delight

THIS IS A MODERN VERSION OF THE CLASSIC POUSSE-CAFÉ, AN UNMIXED, MIXED DRINK, IN THAT THE INGREDIENTS FORM SEPARATE LAYERS IN THE GLASS – PROVIDING YOU HAVE A STEADY HAND. YOU CAN DRINK IT AS A SLAMMER OR SIP IT.

SERVES 1

½ measure chilled grenadine
½ measure chilled Triple Sec
½ measure chilled sloe gin
½ measure chilled single cream

1. Pour the grenadine into a chilled shot or pousse-café glass, then, with a steady hand, pour in the Triple Sec to make a second layer.
2. Add the sloe gin to make a third layer and, finally, add the cream to float on top.

B-52

THE B-52 WAS CREATED IN THE FAMOUS ALICE'S RESTAURANT IN MALIBU, CALIFORNIA. THE NAME REFERS TO THE US B-52 STRATOFORTRESS LONG-RANGE BOMBER.

SERVES 1

1 measure chilled dark crème de cacao
1 measure chilled Baileys Irish Cream
1 measure chilled Grand Marnier

1. Pour the crème de cacao into a shot glass.
2. With a steady hand, gently pour in the Baileys Irish Cream to make a second layer, then gently pour in the Grand Marnier.
3. Cover and slam.

Nuclear Fallout

THIS IS SIMILAR TO A POUSSE-CAFÉ, WHERE THE LIQUEURS ARE LAYERED, BUT, IN THIS CASE, THE HEAVIEST LIQUEUR IS COLDEST AND ADDED LAST, TO CREATE THE SLOW DROPPING EFFECT!

SERVES 1

1 tsp raspberry syrup
¼ measure of maraschino
¼ measure of yellow Chartreuse
¼ measure Cointreau
½ measure well-iced blue Curaçao

1. Chill all the liqueurs but put the blue Curaçao in the coldest part of the freezer. Also chill a shot or pousse-café glass.
2. Carefully pour the drinks in layers over the back of a teaspoon except the blue Curaçao.
3. Finally, pour in the blue Curaçao and wait for the fallout!

Stars and Swirls

YOU WILL NEED A STEADY HAND FOR THIS ONE – PREFERABLY TWO PAIRS OF STEADY HANDS.

SERVES 1

1 measure Malibu
large ice cube
½ measure strawberry or raspberry liqueur
1 tsp blue Curaçao

1. Chill a small shot glass really well.
2. Pour in the Malibu and add a large ice cube.
3. Carefully pour in the other two liqueurs from opposite sides of the glass very slowly so they fall down the sides and swirl around.

Banana Bomber

THIS COCKTAIL IS AS DAZZLING AS IT IS DELICIOUS AND GLORIOUSLY ADDICTIVE. TRY IT WITH WHITE CRÈME DE CACAO AND A LAYER OF CREAM TOO – EQUALLY IRRESISTIBLE!

SERVES 1

1 measure banana liqueur
1 measure brandy

1. Pour the banana liqueur gently into a shot glass.
2. Gently pour in the brandy over the back of a teaspoon, taking care not to let the layers mix.

Fancy Free

THE KEY TO THIS LAYERED DRINK IS TO ICE THE LIQUEUR AND ICE THE GLASS. IF IT DOES SEEM TO MIX ON IMPACT, GIVE IT A LITTLE TIME TO SETTLE AND FORM ITS LAYERS AGAIN.

SERVES 1

⅓ measure cherry brandy, iced

⅓ measure Cointreau, iced

⅓ measure apricot liqueur, iced

1 Into an iced tall shot glass pour the three liqueurs in order. Pour them over the back of a spoon so they form coloured layers.

Fifth Avenue

AFTER-DINNER COCKTAILS OFTEN INCLUDE CREAM AND THIS ONE ALSO HAS THE DELICATE FLAVOURS OF APRICOT AND COCOA.

SERVES 1

1 measure dark crème de cacao, iced
1 measure apricot brandy, iced
1 measure cream

1 Pour the ingredients, one at a time, into a chilled tall glass. Pour the layers slowly over the back of a spoon resting against the edge of the glass. Each layer should float on top of the previous one.

African Mint

AMARULA IS A VERY RICH AND EXOTIC LIQUEUR, WHICH IS BEST SERVED AND DRUNK REALLY COLD – BUT NOT ON ICE AS THAT WILL DILUTE ITS REAL CHARACTER.

SERVES 1

¾ measure crème de menthe, chilled
¾ measure Amarula, chilled

1 Pour the crème de menthe into the base of shot glass, saving a few drops.
2 Pour the Amarula slowly over the back of a spoon to create a layer over the mint.
3 Drizzle any remaining drops of mint over the creamy liqueur to finish.

Napoleon's Nightcap

INSTEAD OF HOT CHOCOLATE, HE FAVOURED A CHOCOLATE-LACED BRANDY WITH A HINT OF BANANA AND MINT. DARING AND EXTRAVAGANT!

SERVES 1

1¼ measures cognac
1 measure dark crème de cacao
¼ measure crème de banane
ice
1 tbsp cream

1. Stir the first three ingredients in a mixing glass with ice.
2. Strain into a chilled cocktail glass and spoon on a layer of cream.

After Five

ORIGINALLY THIS WAS THE NAME OF A MIXED COCKTAIL TOPPED UP WITH LEMONADE OR SODA. IT HAS NOW BEEN COMPLETELY TRANSFORMED INTO A LAYERED SHOOTER WITH A REAL KICK.

SERVES 1

½ measure chilled peppermint schnapps
1 measure chilled Kahlúa
1 tbsp chilled Baileys Irish Cream

1 Pour the peppermint schnapps into a shot glass. Carefully pour the Kahlúa over the back of a teaspoon so that it forms a separate layer. Finally, float the Baileys Irish Cream on top.

The Perfect Shot

Sputnik

IF YOU ARE MAKING SEVERAL OF THESE THEY CAN BE PREPARED IN ADVANCE WITH DIFFERENT COLOURED CHERRIES IN ORBIT ON TOP.

SERVES 1

1 measure vodka
1 measure cream
1 tsp maraschino
ice
maraschino cherry, to decorate

1. Shake all the liquid ingredients well over ice and strain into a glass.
2. Finish with a cherry supported on 2 or more crossed cocktail sticks.

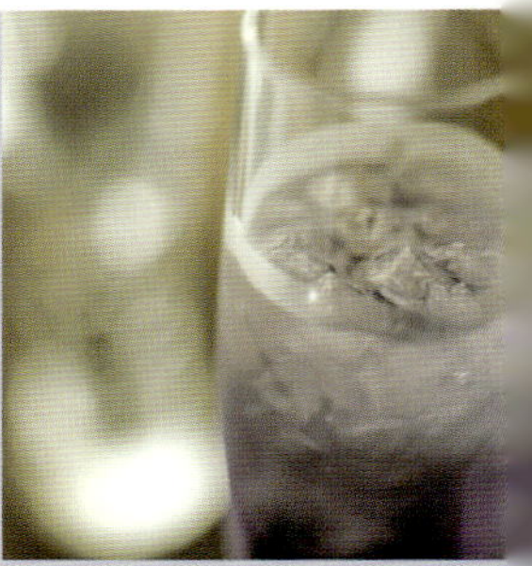

Perfect Love

THIS IS THE LITERAL TRANSLATION FOR AN UNUSUAL PURPLE LIQUEUR FLAVOURED WITH ROSE PETALS, ALMONDS AND VANILLA.

SERVES 1
1 measure vodka
½ measure Parfait Amour
½ measure maraschino
scoop of crushed ice

1. Shake all the ingredients together over ice until frosted.
2. Strain into a chilled shot glass with more ice.

Depth Charge

PERNOD IS A PARTICULARLY UNUSUAL DRINK IN THAT IT TURNS CLOUDY WHEN MIXED WITH WATER BUT NOT WHEN MIXED WITH OTHER ALCOHOLIC DRINKS, UNTIL THE ICE STARTS MELTING. SO DRINK IT SLOWLY, WITH CARE, AND WATCH IT CHANGE.

SERVES 1

1 measure gin
1 measure Lillet
2 dashes Pernod
ice

1. Shake all the liquid ingredients over ice until well frosted.
2. Strain into a chilled shot glass.

Peach Floyd

SHOTS LOOK STUNNING IN THE RIGHT TYPE OF GLASS, BUT AS THEY ARE FOR DRINKING DOWN IN ONE, KEEP THEM SMALL AND HAVE EVERYTHING REALLY WELL CHILLED.

SERVES 1

1 measure peach schnapps, chilled
1 measure vodka, chilled
1 measure white cranberry and peach juice, chilled
1 measure cranberry juice, chilled
ice

1 Stir all the liquid ingredients together over ice and pour into an iced shot glass.

Jealousy

THIS REALLY IS AN AFTER-DINNER COCKTAIL AND IF YOU WANT A CHANGE, YOU COULD OCCASIONALLY FLAVOUR THE CREAM WITH A DIFFERENT LIQUEUR.

SERVES 1

1 tsp crème de menthe
1–2 tbsp double cream
2 measures coffee or chocolate liqueur
crushed ice
chocolate matchsticks, to decorate

1 Gently beat the mint liqueur into the cream until thick.
2 Pour the coffee liqueur into a very small iced glass and carefully spoon on the whipped flavoured cream.
3 Serve with chocolate matchsticks.

Tequila Shot

ACCORDING TO CUSTOM THIS IS THE ONLY WAY TO DRINK NEAT TEQUILA. IT IS OFTEN DESCRIBED AS BEING SMOOTH AND TART, SO ADDING LIME JUICE AND SALT MAY SOUND CONTRADICTORY, BUT IT WORKS!

SERVES 1

1 measure gold tequila
pinch of salt
wedge of lime

1. Pour the tequila into a shot glass.
2. Put the salt at the base of your thumb, between thumb and forefinger.
3. Hold the lime wedge in the same hand.
4. Hold the shot in the other hand.
5. Lick the salt, down the tequila and suck the lime.

Alaska

YELLOW CHARTREUSE IS SLIGHTLY SWEETER THAN GREEN CHARTREUSE, SO IT DOES BENEFIT FROM BEING REALLY WELL CHILLED.

SERVES 1
½ measure gin
½ measure yellow Chartreuse
ice

1 Shake the liquid ingredients over ice until well frosted.
2 Strain into a chilled glass.

Breakfast

IT IS DIFFICULT TO BELIEVE THAT ANYONE WOULD ACTUALLY HAVE THE STOMACH TO COPE WITH COCKTAILS FIRST THING IN THE MORNING – BUT THEN, FOR THOSE WHO PARTY ALL NIGHT AND SLEEP ALL DAY, COCKTAIL TIME COINCIDES WITH BREAKFAST.

SERVES 1

2 measures gin
1 measure grenadine
cracked ice cubes
1 egg yolk

1 Pour the gin and grenadine over ice in a shaker and add the egg yolk.

2 Shake vigorously until frosted. Strain into a chilled glass.

Voodoo

THIS ENTHRALLING MIXTURE OF FLAVOURS IS GUARANTEED TO WEAVE A SPELL ON YOUR TASTE BUDS AND WORK ITS MAGIC FROM THE VERY FIRST SIP.

SERVES 1

½ measure chilled Kahlúa
½ measure chilled Malibu
½ measure chilled butterscotch schnapps
1 measures chilled milk

1 Pour the Kahlúa, Malibu, schnapps and milk into a glass and stir well.

Whiskey Sour Jelly Shot

A NEW TWIST ON A CLASSIC COCKTAIL FOR A NEW GENERATION OF COCKTAIL DRINKERS, BUT BE CAREFUL TO KEEP CHILDREN AWAY FROM THE REFRIGERATOR.

SERVES 10
1 packet lemon jelly
300 ml/10 fl oz hot water
225–300 ml/8–10 fl oz Scotch whisky

1 Break up the jelly and place it in a heatproof measuring jug. Pour in the hot water and stir until the jelly has dissolved. Leave until cool, then stir in the whisky to make the mixture up to 600 ml/ 1 pint.
2 Divide among 8 shot glasses and chill in the refrigerator until set. Once set remove from the refrigerator and eat with spoon.

Margarita Jelly Shot

IT IS NOT ESSENTIAL TO FROST THE GLASSES WITH SALT BUT IT DOES LOOK ATTRACTIVE AND PAYS HOMAGE TO THE ORIGINAL NON-JELLY COCKTAIL RECIPE OF 1942.

SERVES 10

½ lime, cut into wedges
2 tbsp fine salt
1 packet lime jelly
300 ml/10 fl oz hot water
4–5 tbsp Cointreau
200–250 ml/7–9 fl oz tequila

1. Rub the outside rims of 10 shot glasses with the lime wedges, then dip in the salt to frost them. Set aside.
2. Break up the jelly and place it in a heatproof measuring jug. Pour in the hot water and stir until the jelly has dissolved. Leave until cool, then stir in the Cointreau and tequila to make the mixture up to 600 ml/1 pint.
3. Divide among the prepared shot glasses, taking care not to disturb the salt frosting, and chill in the refrigerator until set.

Peppermint Patty

SOMETIMES THE SIMPLE THINGS IN LIFE ARE THE BEST AND THIS PERFECT COMBINATION OF CHOCOLATE AND PEPPERMINT IS JUST SUCH A ONE.

SERVES 1

cracked ice

1 measure white crème de cacao

1 measure white crème de menthe

1 Put the ice in a cocktail shaker and pour in the crème de cacao and crème de menthe. Close the shaker and shake vigorously for 10–20 seconds, until the outside of the shaker is misted. Strain into a shot glass.

Prairie Oyster

WHEN YOU REALLY CAN'T LIFT YOUR HEAD OFF THE PILLOW, IT'S THE ONLY THING TO TRY.

SERVES 1
Worcestershire sauce
vinegar
tomato ketchup
1 egg yolk
cayenne pepper, to decorate

1. Mix equal quantities of Worcestershire sauce, vinegar and ketchup and pour into a chilled glass.
2. Add the yolk carefully without breaking.
3. Do not stir, sprinkle with cayenne pepper and down it all in one!

Hair of the Dog

THIS WELL-KNOWN EXPRESSION – A TOT OF WHATEVER GAVE YOU THE HANGOVER – IS IN FACT A POPULAR SCOTTISH 'MORNING AFTER' TIPPLE!

SERVES 1

1 measure Scotch whisky
1½ measures single cream
½ measure clear honey
ice

1 Gently mix the whisky, cream and honey together.
2 Pour into a shot glass over ice and serve.

Zipper

THIS SHOOTER GETS ITS NAME FROM AN UNUSUAL, NOT TO SAY 'LOUCHE METHOD' OF SERVING IT, BUT TASTES JUST AS GOOD SERVED MORE CONVENTIONALLY.

SERVES 1
crushed ice
1 measure tequila
½ measure Grand Marnier
½ measure single cream

1 Put the crushed ice into a cocktail shaker and pour in the tequila, Grand Marnier and cream. Close the shaker and shake vigorously for 10–20 seconds, until the outside of the shaker is misted. Strain into a shot glass.

index

Enjoy the walks, and may the sun shine all day, your boots feel comfortable on your feet and your pack feels as light as a feather!
Happy walking!
John N. Merrill

Something to ponder.

As we walk around this amazing world, we take for granted the stunning diversity of life and nature. We pass the slopes of mountains and the river valleys. We see birds, insects, animals and all the kaleidoscope of flowers and trees. But let's stop for a moment and just stand in awe of this plethora of sights. However hard we, as humans try, we cannot match the magnificence that our eyes see. Whether you are spiritual or not, you cannot ignore or be moved to wonder at the incredible work of a higher dimension - the divine.

While many would say this is evolution, there still has be "someone", who first thought up the flower, tree, bird, animal, and landscape. You only have to gaze at a small mountain flower and see the delicate stems and petals made to perfection. Whilst the earth's movement have created our landscape, the forces of the divine have been at work to help create that breathtaking view. We on the other-hand have been given eyes and feelings, so that we can appreciate and stand in awe at the sight before us.

So as we wander down a path in woodland or high mountains, where the whole spectrum of life is laid out for us to see. Lets give eternal thanks for being able to walk and see these things first hand. To be able to touch, feel and appreciate the work of the divine, makes the effort more than worthwhile. So, as you walk, stop and ponder at the never ending variety of sights and smells that confront us on each stride we take.

John N. Merrill 2014

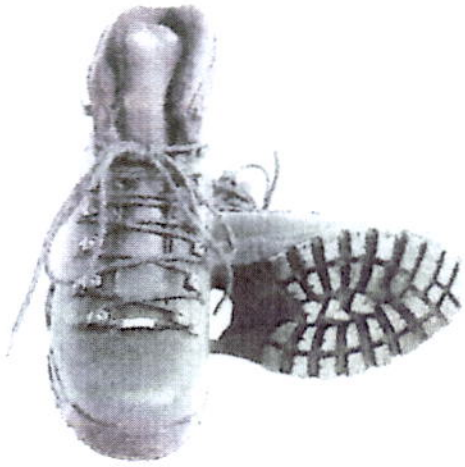

A walker.

There is a walker
who in his youth walked
up hill and down dale.
As the years passed he
went for longer walks,
not 20 or 30 miles or
even 100 miles,
but walks of a minimum of
1,000 miles.
He progressed to 1,500 miles,
then 2,100 miles and knew
he was ready for the big one.
7,000 miles around Britain.
He then left these shores
and did long walks in
Europe, America and Asia.
So far has done more than
219,500 miles and written
450 books, while wearing
out 134 pairs of boots.
He has never been ill,
or broken a bone or been
in hospital.
He has had no new knees or
hips, he is in the same body
that he was born with.
Who is this man?
Why me, Revd. John Merrill!

(Copyright - JNM October 31st. 2017)

OTHER JOHN MERRILL DAY CHALLENGE WALKS -

WHITE PEAK CHALLENGE WALK
THE HAPPY HIKER - WHITE PEAK - CHALLENGE WALK No.2
DARK PEAK CHALLENGE WALK
PEAK DISTRICT END TO END WALKS
STAFFORDSHIRE MOORLANDS CHALLENGE WALK
THE LITTLE JOHN CHALLENGE WALK
YORKSHIRE DALES CHALLENGE WALK
NORTH YORKSHIRE MOORS CHALLENGE WALK
LAKELAND CHALLENGE WALK
THE RUTLAND WATER CHALLENGE WALK
MALVERN HILLS CHALLENGE WALK
THE SALTER'S WAY
THE SNOWDON CHALLENGE
CHARNWOOD FOREST CHALLENGE WALK
THREE COUNTIES CHALLENGE WALK (Peak District).
CAL-DER-WENT WALK
THE QUANTOCK WAY
BELVOIR WITCHES CHALLENGE WALK
THE CARNEDDAU CHALLENGE WALK
THE SWEET PEA CHALLENGE WALK
THE LINCOLNSHIRE WOLDS - BLACK DEATH - CHALLENGE WALK
JENNIFER'S CHALLENGE WALK
THE EPPING FOREST CHALLENGE WALK
THE THREE BOROUGH CHALLENGE WALK - NORTH LONDON
THE HERTFORD CHALLENGE WALK
THE BOSHAM CHALLENGE WALK
NORFOLK BROADS CHALLENGE WALK
THE KING JOHN CHALLENGE WALK
THE SURREY HILLS CHALLENGE WALK
THE RIVER MIMRAM CHALLENGE WALK
THE BRIGHTON WAY
THE ISLE OF THANET CHALLENGE WALK
THE RIVER WEY & GODALMING NAVIGATIONS
EAST DEVON CHALLENGE WALK

HELP ME TO KEEP THE WALK GUIDES UPTO DATE.

This guidebook instructions were correct when written and I have detailed what I have found on my walk. But the countryside changes - stiles become kissing gates; inns change their names or are closed down. Paths are diverted, new roads are made, and path signs are often vandalised.

I endeavour to keep upto date with the changes but with about 450 guidebooks covering some 8,600 routes it is a never ending task. I do completely rewalk the routes and write totally new books about a specific walk or route, but it takes time. If you do one of the walks in this book and you find an error or an amendment, would you inform me? The update will be added to book immediately and you will receive a signed copy of the updated book, as a thank you gift.

Your help is greatly appreciated.

Happy walking!
John
Email - marathonhiker@aol.com

The John Merrill Foundation

- is a not for profit charitable Foundation, solely committed to ensuring the copyright, moral rights and writings of Revd. John Merrill are available to all.

The book was originally published by John Merrill and went through numerous reprintings. This Print-on-Demand edition was first printed in 2017.

All rights reserved.

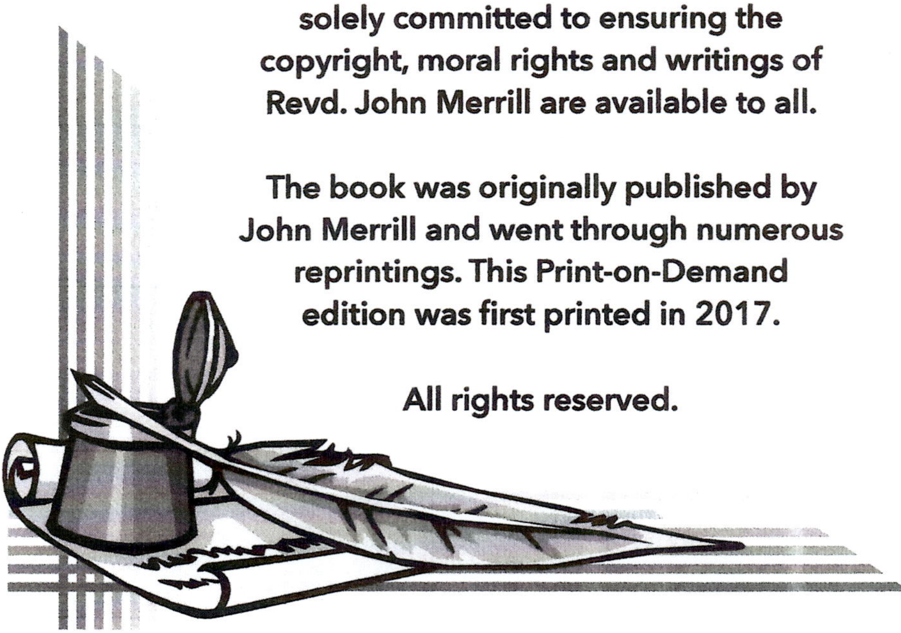

Walking the Streets of LONDON

by Revd. John N. Merrill

THE JOHN MERRILL FOUNDATION

THE JOHN MERRILL FOUNDATION
32, Holmesdale, Waltham Cross, Hertfordshire, England. EN8 8QY

Tel/Fax - 01992-762776
E-mail - john@johnmerrillwalkguides.co.uk
www. johnmerrillwalkguides.co.uk
www.thejohnmerrillministry.co.uk
www.londoninterfaithchurch.co.uk

International Copyright © John Merrill . All rights reserved. No part of this publication may be reproduced or transmitted in any form or by any means electronic or mechanical including photocopy, recording or any information storage or retrieval system in any place, in any country without the prior written permission of The John Merrill Foundation.

John N. Merrill asserts their moral rights to be identified as the authors of this work.

A catalogue record for this book is available from the British Library.

Conceived, edited, typset and designed by *The John Merrill Foundation*
Printed and handmade by ***John N. Merrill.***
Book layout and cover design by ***John N. Merrill***

© Text and photographs - by Revd. John N. Merrill 2013
© Maps by Revd. John N. Merrill, HonMUniv, R.I.M.A. 2013
© Additional material - Revd. John N. Merrill, HonMUniv, 2013.

ISBN 978 - 0-9553691-1-7
First Published - July 2006. Reprinted and revised - March 2013.
Special limited edition.

Typeset in Humanst521 - bold, italic, and plain 11pt, 14pt and 18pt
Main titles in 18pt .**Humanst521 Bd BT** by John Merrill in Adobe Pagemaker on a iMac.

Please note - *The maps in this guide are purely illustrative. You are encouraged to use the appropriate 1:25,000 O.S. Explorer map as detailed on each walk.*

John Merrill confirms he has walked all the routes in this book and detailed what he found. Meticulous research has been undertaken to ensure that this publication is highly accurate at the time of going to press. The publishers, however, cannot be held responsible for alterations, errors, omissions, or for changes in details given. They would welcome information to help keep the book up to date.

Cover design & photo's © The John Merrill Foundation 2013.

Photographs by Revd. John N. Merrill.

The John Merrill Foundation maintains the John Merrill Library and archives and administers the worldwide pubishing rights of John Merrill's works in all media formats.

Printed on paper from a 100% sustainable forest.
The John Merrill Foundation plants sufficient trees through the Woodland Trust to replenish the trees used in its publications.

John high up the Lake District - June 2017.

A little about Revd. John N. Merrill

John is unique, possessing the skills of a marathon runner, mountain climber and athlete. Since his first 1,000 mile walk through the islands of the Inner and Outer Hebrides in 1970, he has since walked over 219,000 miles and worn out 133 pairs of boots, 49 rucksacks and more than 1,600 pairs of socks. He has brought marathon walking to Olympic standard. In 1978 he became the first person to walk around the entire coastline of Britain - 7,000 miles. He has walked across Europe, the Alps and Pyrenees - 3,000 miles with 600,000 feet of ascent and descent. In America he has walked the 2,500 mile Appalachian Trail; the Pacific Crest Trail - 2,500 miles in record time; the Continental Divide Trail; became the first person to thru-hike the Buckeye Trail - 1,350 miles in Ohio and completed a unique 4,260 mile walk in 178 days coast to coast across America. He has climbed all the mountains in New Mexico and walked all the trails.

In Britain he has walked all the National Trails many times; linked all the National Parks and trails in a 2,060 mile walk; completed a 1,608 mile Land's End to John o' Groats walk and countless other unique walks. He has walked three times to Santiago de Compostella via different routes; to St. Olav's Shrine in Norway - 420 miles; walked to Assisi, St. Gilles du Gard, the Cathar Ways and to Mont St. Michel. He has walked every long distance path in France and Germany, and walked to every pilgrimage destination in England and France, and extensively walked in every country in Europe.

He has walked in Africa; all the trails in the Hong Kong Islands; and completed five trekking expeditions to the Himalyas and India. Not only is he the world's leading marathon walker he is Britain's most experienced walker. John is author of more than 440 walk guides which have sold more than 4 million copies with more than 1 million sold on the Peak District. He has created more than 80 challenge walks which have been used to raise, so far, more than a £1 million for different charities.

John has never broken a bone or been lost and never had any trouble anywhere. He still walks in the same body he was born with, has had no replacements and does not use poles. This he puts down to his deep spiritual nature and in 2010 he was ordained as a multi-faith Minister - a universal monk, "honouring and embracing all faiths and none". He conducts weddings and funerals services all over UK and abroad. He teaches Qigong and is a Reiki practioner. He gives illustrated talks on his walks all over the U.K.

CONTENTS

Household Cavalry - Horse Guard Parade, Whitehall.
See the "Good and Gracious Walk."

INTRODUCTION

Here are seven walks - a full week of walking - exploring many of historical and key features found in central London. Whilst not long in terms of distance, they contain many places to explore, so a 3 mile walk could take six hours, depending on your interest. Basically each walk explores a specific theme - such as the Great Fire of 1666 - but as you walk along you will see much, much more and it is for you to decide how long you take and what you visit. They are not to hurried but simply to "stroll" and explore the architecture, the stories, the buildings and the museums that you pass.

My passport states I was born in London but I wasn't there long. Over the years I visited and saw the Houses of Parliament and Buckingham Palace, but it was many years later that I started to walk the streets of London. Looking from a different perspective, I wanted to learn her secrets and discover her history on the ground. I wanted no preconceived ideas or information. I just wanted to set off and learn.

These seven walks are my walks of discovery and what I found on the way, from the well known to lesser known. They have brought me much enjoyment and pride as I saw places where English history was made through the centuries.

Set off and enjoy for yourself this large but absorbing city, whether you are a visitor or local, for both of you will be amazed at what there is to see. This book is finished but the walking goes on, for the more you learn, the more you discover, and want to see.

Enjoy and

Happy walking

ABOUT CITY WALKING
- some personal thoughts.

Whilst every care is taken detailing and describing the walks in this book, it should be borne in mind that the countryside changes by the seasons and the work of man. I have described the walk to the best of my ability, detailing what I have found on the walk in the way of stiles and signs. Obviously with the passage of time stiles become broken or replaced by a ladder stile or even a small gate. Signs too have a habit of being broken, pushed over or obliterated by graffiti. All the route follow rights of way and only on rare occasions will you have to overcome obstacles in its path, such as a temporary closed path because of repair work. On rare occasions rights of way are re-routed and these amendments are included in the next edition. Inns have a frustrating time of changing their name, then back to the original one!

The seasons bring occasional problems whilst out walking which should also be borne in mind. In the height of summer countryside paths can become overgrown and you may have to fight your way through in a few places. In summer the ground is generally dry but in autumn and winter, especially because of our climate, the surface can be decidedly wet and slippery; sometimes even gluttonous mud!

These comments are part of countryside walking which help to make your walk more interesting or briefly frustrating. Standing up to your ankles in mud might not be funny at the time but upon reflection was one of the highlights of the walk!

The mileage for each section is based on three calculations -

1. pedometer reading.
2. the route map measured on the map.
3. the time I took for the walk.

I believe the figure stated for each section to be very accurate but we all walk differently and not always in a straight line! The time allowed for each walk is on the generous side and does not include any sight seeing, refreshment stops or pub stops. The figure is based on the fact that on average a person walks 3 miles an hours but less in hilly terrain. Allow 20 minutes to walk a mile; ten minutes for 1/2 mile and five minutes for 1/4 mile.

Walking in the London area is naturally flat and a good public transport system operates. On most walks you are never far from a bus stop or underground/ train station. If you feel you have had enough and only done part of the walk; stop and go home and come back another day. There is no shame in only doing part of the walk; it is better to have walked part of it than not at all.

CITY WALKING EQUIPMENT NOTES - some personal thoughts.

Today there is a bewildering variety of walking gear, much is superfluous to general walking in Britain. As a basic observation, people over dress for the outdoors. Basically equipment should be serviceable and do the task. I don't approve of walking poles; humans were built to walk with two legs! The following are some of my throughts gathered from my unique walking experiences.

FOOTWEAR - For summer use I wear walking trainers and in winter lightweight boots. I prefer a good quality boot with a full leather upper, of medium weight, with a vibram sole. I always add a foam cushioned insole to help cushion the base of my feet.

SOCKS - I generally wear two thick pairs as this helps minimise blisters. The inner pair are of loop stitch variety and approximately 80% wool. The outer are a thick rib pair of approximately 80% wool.

CLOTHES & WATERPROOFS - for general walking I wear a T shirt or cotton shirt with a cotton wind jacket on top, and shorts - even in snow! You generate heat as you walk and I prefer to layer my clothes to avoid getting too hot. Depending on the season will dictate how many layers you wear. In soft rain I just use my wind jacket for I know it quickly dries out. In heavy or consistant rain I slip on a poncho, which covers my pack and allows air to circulate, while keeping dry. Only in extreme conditions will I don overtrousers, much preferring to get wet and feel comfortable. I never wear gaiters!

FOOD - as I walk I carry bars of chocolate, for they provide instant energy and are light to carry. In winter a flask of hot coffee is welcome. I never carry water and find no hardship from not doing so, but this is a personal matter! From experience I find the more I drink the more I want and sweat. You should always carry some extra food such as trail mix & candy bars etc., for emergencies.

RUCKSACKS - for day walking I use a climbing rucksack of about 40 litre capacity and although it leaves excess space it does mean that the sac has a well padded back, padded shoulder straps, and a raincover. Inside apart from the basics for one day, including a camera, in winter I carry gloves, spare pullover and a pair of socks.

MAP - when I am walking I always have the relevant map - preferably 1:25,000 scale - open in my hand. This enables me to constantly check that I am walking the right way.

THE ROYAL PALACES WALK - 6 1/2 MILES - HYDE PARK MAP

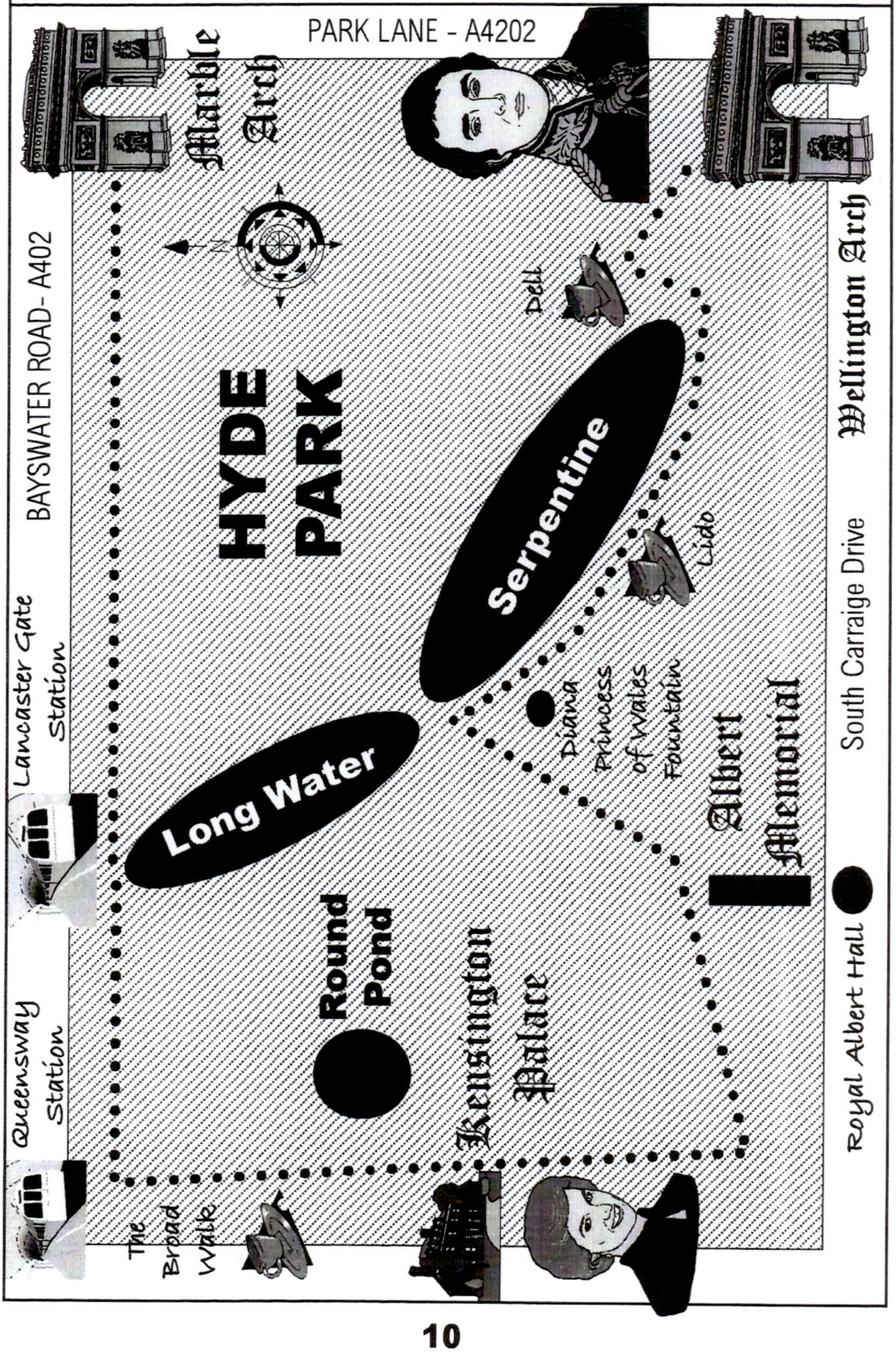

THE ROYAL PALACES WALK
- 6 1/2 MILES
- allow 3 to 4 hours

Basic route - Marble Arch Underground Station - Hyde Park - Kensington Palace - Albert Memorial - Diana, Princess of Wales, Memorial Fountain - Serpentine - Serpentine Road - Hyde Park Corner - Wellington Arch - Constitution Hill - Buckingham Palace - Birdcage Walk - Guards' Chapel & Museum - St. James's Park - Horse Guards Parade - The Mall - St. James Palace - Green Park - Spencer House - Green Park Underground Station.

Start - Marble Arch Underground Station - Central Line.
End - Green Park Underground Station - Piccadilly/Victoria & Jubilee Lines.

Cafe's - Three in Hyde Park. Others in St. James's Park and Green Park. You can also hire deck chairs in all the parks.

Full amenities at Green Park - Piccadilly Road.

ABOUT THE WALK - The basic theme is Royal Palaces, as you pass Kensington Palace, Buckingham Palace, Clarence House and St. James's Palace. You see the splendour of the Monarchy and most places associated with its rich pageantry. If you start early enough - 9. 30 a.m. - you should arrive at Buckingham Palace at 11.30 a.m. to watch the changing of the guards; a splendid ceremony best seen from the gates area of Buckingham Palace or from the steps of the Queen Victoria Memorial. You also walk through three of London's premier Royal Parks; see Princess Diana's former home and her memorial fountain; the Albert Memorial with the circular Royal Albert Hall behind; Wellington's Archway and Apsley House closeby; the ceremonial parade area of the Mall and Horse Guards Parade; the former home of the Queen Mother and St. James's Palace; and finally and aptly, the Spencer House. Like all these walks in this book, there is much to see and places/museums to visit; it is upto you how long you spend on the walk - you could spend the morning only or the whole day.

WALKING INSTRUCTIONS - From Marble Arch Underground Station follow the signs to Exit 9 for Hyde Park; visit Marble Arch, Speakers Corner and the site of the Tyburn Tree, on the way.

MARBLE ARCH - ***Designed by John Nash in 1827. Originally situated infront of Buckingham Palace but in 1851 was moved to here, as it was thought not to be grand enough. By law, only the royal family are allowed to walk through the centre. Inside is a one bed roomed flat, a stark contrast to homeless that sleep nearby.***

SPEAKER'S CORNER - ***The only place in Britain, since 1872, where protesters can meet without police approval. Here many people will stand on a soap box and extol their beliefs, to the uninterested passers-by. Situated near Marble Arch, roadside.***

TYBURN TREE - ***For nearly 500 years a three legged gallows stood here and some 50,000 people were executed; the last in 1783. A plaque in the road marks the spot. Close by at 8, Hyde Park Place is the Tyburn Convent, where more than 100 Catholic martyrs are buried. Open daily; free admission.***

HYDE PARK - ***London's largest park - 145 hectares. Carpeted in flowers in the Spring and popular with sunbathers in the summer; you can hire deck chairs. Horse rides, gun salutes, pop concerts all take place here. For a while it was a Royal hunting park in the 16th. century and in the early 17th. century became the first royal park opened to the public. The Serpentine lake was made in the mid 18th. century. You can hire boats on the lake and beside it are cafe's. The grey squirrels are very tame!***

The fountains and start of Long Water; Hyde Park.

Walk through the subway to Hyde Park and turn right; you basically keep to the northern side of the park for the next 1 1/2 miles. In nearly 1/2 mile reach Victoria Gate, and keep right then left to continue along the northern side to pass the fountains and start of the Long Water on your left; away to your right is Lancaster Gate Underground Station. You will no doubt have noticed that the grey squirrels in the park are very tame. In another 1/2 mile reach the Queensway Underground Station and Hilton Hotel on your right. Turn left here on a wide surfaced road - The Broad Walk. Soon pass on the right a tea-room at Elfin Oak and Princess Diana Memorial Gardens, for children, opened 30th. June 2000. Soon after on the right is The Orangery and entrance to the State Apartments of Kensington Palace.

Kensington Palace.

KENSINGTON PALACE - ***Bought by William 3rd. (better known as William of Orange - his statue can be seen through the front gates) and Mary 2nd. in 1689. Several Monarchs have lived here over the years including Queen Anne, George 1st. and George 2nd. Queen Victoria was born here in 1819. More recently it was the home of Diana, Princess of Wales.***

Continue on The Broad Walk and pass a monument to Victoria 1837 on the right and to the left is the Round Pond. Shortly after bear right on a path to reach the front gates of Kensington Palace, the surrounding area was awash with flowers following the sudden death of Princess Diana. Turn left at the gates along the diagonal path and turn half left at the end to begin walking along the southern side of Hyde Park. Soon to your right is Queens Gate and keep straight ahead on the path through the "garden" to the Albert Memorial on your right, with the Royal Albert Hall beyond.

The Albert Memorial and the dome of the Abert Hall.

THE ALBERT MEMORIAL - *Regarded as the finest monument of the Victorian era, it recently underwent a £11.2 million restoration. Named after Queen Victoria's husband, Albert (1819-1861).*

ROYAL ALBERT HALL - *Built in 1871 and famous for the annual BBC Promenade concerts (Henry Wood).*

From the rear of the memorial follow the path which soon curves left. At a path junction keep straight ahead to pass the Serpentine Gallery - the park is well signed posted. Before the bridge over The Serpentine, turn right along its southern side to Princess Diana's Memorial Fountain.

DIANA MEMORIAL FOUNTAIN - ***Opened by Queen Elizabeth 2nd in the 6th. July 2004. Said to reflect the peacefulness and life of Princess Diana, the water flows in two directions to the bottom, along channels and waterfalls. The circular fountain is made from 545 pieces of Cornish Granite.***

Continue beside The Serpentine to the Lido Cafe and the famous Serpentine Swimming Club; it is these brave souls who swim on January 1st. each year; sometimes breaking the ice! Continue by the The Serpentine to its end and turn left over a bridge. Just before it is a memorial to Queen Caroline, wife of George 2nd.

"To the memory of
Queen Caroline
wife of George I I
for whom
The Long Water
and Serpentine
were created
between
1727 - 1731".

On the otherside of the bridge is another memorial marking the start of a water conduit to the Abbey of Westminster by King Edward the Confessor. Renewed in 1536 and by Queen Elizabeth 1st by charter in 1560. Pass the Dell Cafe on your left and turn right, along Serpentine Road. Soon on your left is the bandstand and shortly afterwards the Cavalry of the Empire Memorial. At the end of the road reach Hyde Park Corner - the tube station is to your right.

Cross the road aiming for Wellington Arch. To your left is Apsley House and a memorial to the Duke of Wellington. On the right is a large monument to the Royal Artillery, who between 1914 - 1919 lost 49,076 lives. Just before the arch on the right is the Australian War Memorial.

ASPLEY HOUSE - ***Has the pre-eminent address in London - "Number 1, London." The home of the first Duke of Wellington, whose descendant still reside here today. The stunning interior has a display of his life and collections of paintings, porcelain and furniture.***
Open Tuesday to Saturday, all year.

WELLINGTON ARCH - ***Originally planned as an impressive approach to Buckingham Palace. The bronze sculpture - an angel of peace descending on the chariot of war - is the largest in Europe. Open the public who can take the lift to the balcony for impressive views over this area of London.***
Open- Wednesday to Sunday, all year.

THE ROYAL PALACES WALK - 6 1/2 MILES - BUCKINGHAM PALACE & ST. JAMES PALACE - MAP

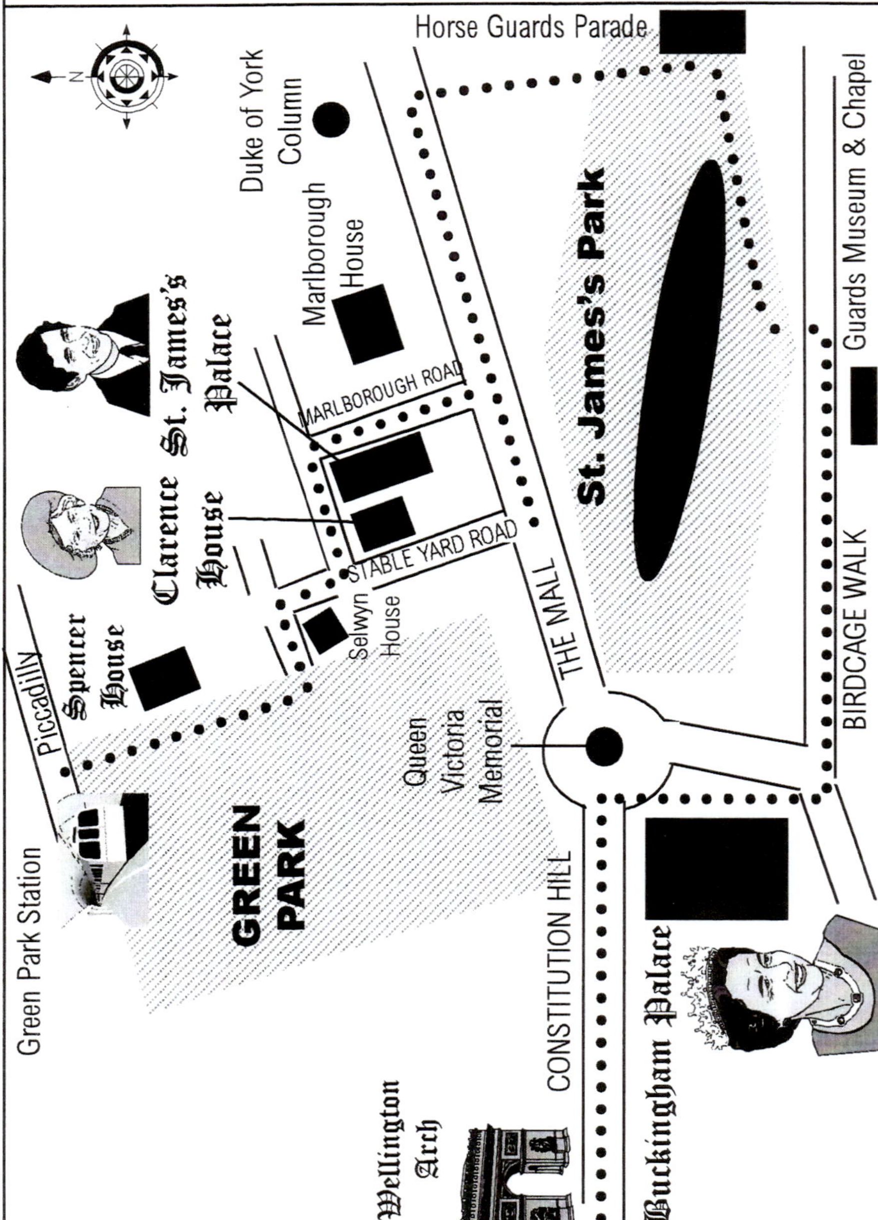

Wellington Arch.

Cross the road into Constitution Hill, and walk on the lefthand side, and immediately pass the Memorial Gates - A debt of Honour for both World Wars when five million men and women of the Indian sub continent, Africa and Caribbean, lost their lives. Continue to Buckingham Palace and the Queen Victoria Memorial.

BUCKINGHAM PALACE - ***Built in 1705 for the Duke of Buckingham. Has been the royal family's London home since 1837.***

QUEEN VICTORIA MEMORIAL - ***25 m. circular monument infront of Buckingham Palace.***

The changing of the Guard ceremony - Buckingham Palace.

CHANGING OF THE GUARD - ***Officially known as, "Guards Mounting", the Foot Guards of the Household Regiment, in their red jackets and bearskin hats, march from their nearby Wellington Barracks and replace the guard's going off duty. The ceremony mostly takes place in the forecourt of Buckingham Palace. The new and old guards march past Queen Victoria's Memorial. Takes place daily at 11.30 a.m. - April to July and the remainder of the year on alternate days.***

To your left is The Mall which you will be walking along later. First keep right past the end of St. James's Park and left along Birdcage Walk. Pass the Wellington Barracks and then the Guards Museum and Chapel. Just at Queen Anne's Gate, turn left into St. James's Park.

GUARDS MUSEUM AND CHAPEL - ***The story and history of the foot guards, dating back to the 17th. century. Inside are many uniforms and considerable memorabilia of their service.***
Open daily.

ST. JAMES'S PARK - ***Beautiful park with a lake, full of flowers and birds, with views to Buckingham Palace and Westminster.***

Immediately turn right to keep to the southern side of the park. Follow the path as it curves left past the end of the lake on your left and pass on the right the Household Cavalry Memorial and Horse Guards Parade beyond.

HORSE GUARDS PARADE - ***The mounted troopers of the Household Cavalry change guard here daily at 11.0 a.m., weekdays and at 10.0. a.m. on Sunday's. The main parade area is the scene for much pageantry and spectacle including the annual Trooping of the Colour, in June to celebrates the Queen's birthday.***

Continue on the path along the edge of the park to The Mall with the Duke of York monument and steps opposite. Turn left along The Mall, passing Carlton House, where the Privy Council meet and Marlborough House. Just after is Marlborough Road - your first road on the right, opposite Marlborough Gate into St. James's Park. You will walk along here shortly but first continue along The Mall, with Buckingham Palace ahead to the next road on your right - Stable Yard Road. There is no access into here but from the gates you can see

CLARENCE HOUSE - ***built by John Nash in 1825-1827, the former home of the Queen Mother, and from this entranceway would appear on her birthday. Here Prince Charles now resides. Beyond is -***

ST, JAMES'S PALACE - ***which dates from 1532/3. The former home of Prince Charles.***

St. James Palace entrance.

Retrace your steps back to Marlborough Road and turn left. Pass Friary Court on the left and Marlborough House - designed by Christopher Wren 1709 - 1711 - on the right. At the end turn left to pass the guarded entrance to St. James's Palace. Continue a little further and turn right then left at Little James's Street, and walk past the righthand side of Selwyn House to the roads end and entrance into Green Park. Turn right along along its righthand side on a wide path and soon pass Spencer House on the right.

Spencer House.

SPENCER HOUSE - ***Built by the first Earl Spencer, 1755-6 - an ancestor of Diana, Princess of Wales.***

GREEN PARK - ***Like the other royal parks it was once a popular duelling area and during World War I I, was planted with potatoes and vegetables.***

Continue on the path past a tea-room to Ritz Corner and Piccadilly Road. To the left is Green Park Underground Station and to the right The Ritz Hotel.

THE GOOD AND THE GRACIOUS - 3 MILES

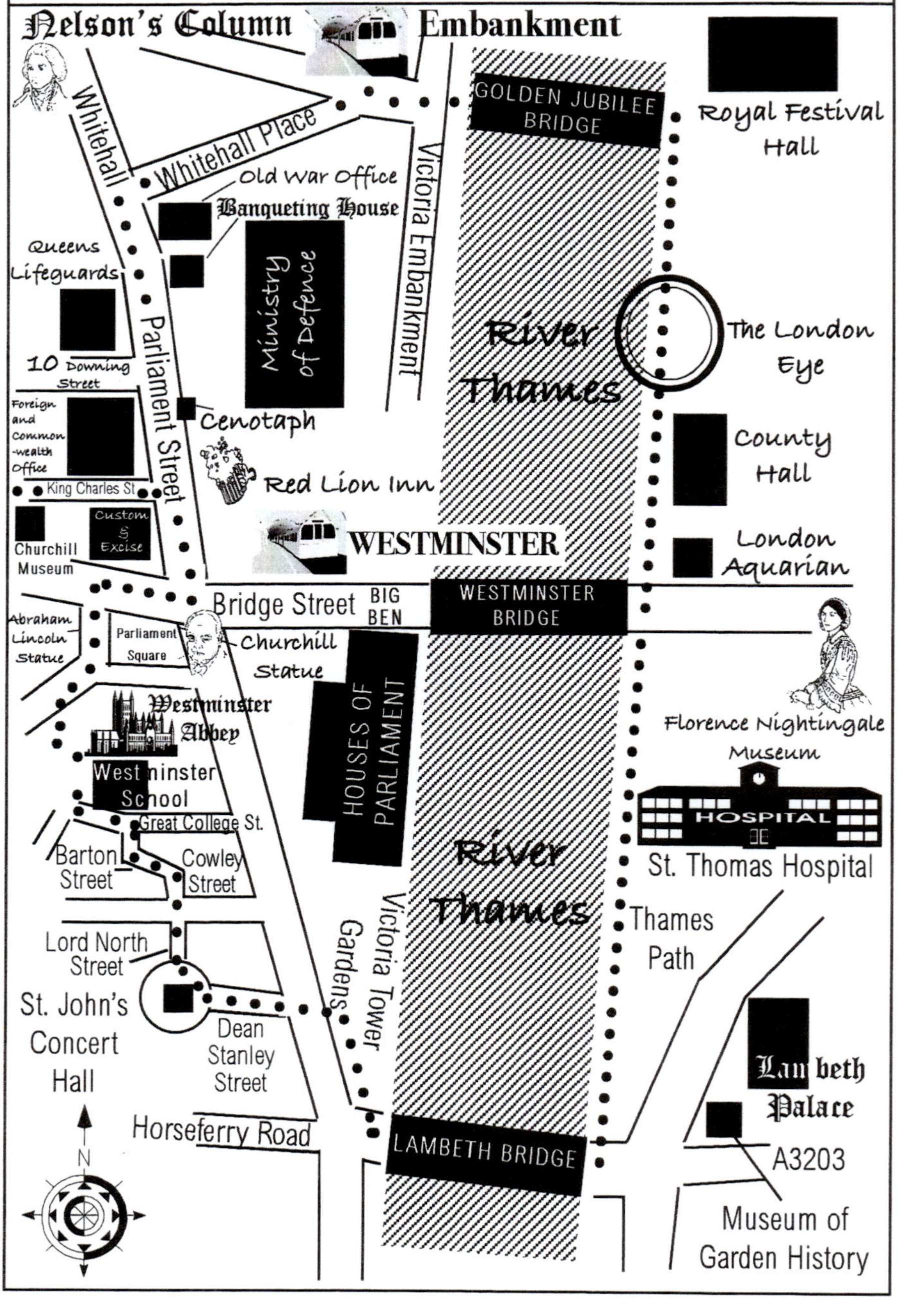

THE GOOD AND THE GRACIOUS - 3 MILES - allow 3 to 4 hours.

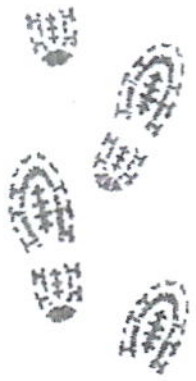

Basic route - Westminster Underground Station - Whitehall - Banqueting Hall Embankment - Golden Jubilee Bridge - Jubilee gardens - London Eye - County hall - Westminster Bridge - St. Thomas Hospital - Lambeth Palace - Lambeth Bridge - Thames path - Victoria Tower Gardens - St. John's Concert hall - Barton Street - Westminster School - Westminster Abbey - St. Margaret's Church - Parliament Square - Houses of Parliament - Westminster Underground Station.

Start and end - Westminster Underground Station.

Inns - Red Lion Inn, Parliament Street.

Cafe's - Hispaniola boat at Embankment (Cafe, bar & restaurant). Numerous along the southern side of the Thames - between the London Eye and London Aquarium. Also others near the Westminster and Embankment Underground Stations.

ABOUT THE WALK - The theme is famous people and politicians, but this is only part of the huge variety of places to be seen on this walk. You will see many statues and memorials; the Cenotaph; the Queen's Life Guards; No. 10 Downing Street; where Kings and Queen were Crowned and where one lost his head! You will cross bridges giving excellent views of the Houses of Parliament and Big Ben; pass the London Eye; Dali Exhibition and the London Aquarium. You pass St. Thomas Hospital and museum to Florence Nightingale; Lambeth Palace, the residence of the Archbishop of Canterbury; and walk along delightful streets close to Westminster School and Abbey. Finally you reach Parliament Square and its important statues and Big Ben. With passing so many important places you could easily spend the whole day visiting the museums and churches along the way - just pick and chose as you pass.

WALKING INSTRUCTIONS - Exit Westminster Underground Station by following the Bridge Street signs. Gaining the road - Bridge Street - opposite is the Houses of Parliament and Big Ben. Turn right and right again along Parliament Street; on your left is Parliament Square and the Churchill Statue - your return route. On the lefthand side of the road is the Treasury - Customs and Excise. A short distance later to your left is King Charles Street; at the end is the Churchill Museum and Cabinet War Rooms.

CHURCHILL MUSEUM AND CABINET WAR ROOMS - ***The greatest Briton of the 20th. century, who led us to victory, from here, in World War I I. But that is only part of the story of this multi talented and extraordinary man, as the museum attempts to explain. Well worth a visit. Open daily.***

Continue along Parliament Street and pass the Red Lion Inn and the Dept. of Health (Richmond House) and the Cenotaph Memorial for two world wars. (Wreath laying ceremony -November I I th.), in the middle of the road on your left. Just after on your left is 10, Downing Street. Now on your right is the Ministry of Defence, built in 1957, and three statues to famous Army Field Marshall's -

Monty - Field Marshall Viscount Montgomery of Alamein KG GCB DSO - 1887-1976.

Field Marshall The Viscount Alan Brooke Kg GCB OM GCVO DSO
"Master of Strategy"
Chief of Imperial General Staff - 1941 - 1946
Master Gunner - St. James park. 1946 - 1956

Field Marshall The Viscount Slim KG GCB GCMG GCVO GBE DSO MC
14th. Army of Burma - 1943 - 1945
Governor General & Commander in Chief Australia 1953 - 1960
Governor & Constable Windsor Castle.

Opposite in the middle of the road is a memorial to the Women of World War I I. Pass the Wales Office on your right and Scottish Office on the left. Then Earl Haig monument in the middle of the road -

Field Marshall Earl Haig -
Commander-in-Chief of the British Armies in France.

The Women of World War I I Memorial.

Next pass the Banqueting House on the right -

The only surviving part of Whitehall Palace, much of it being razed to the ground during a fire in 1698. The building is one of the first Classical Style in Britain, being designed by Indigo James in 1619. In 1635 King Charles 1st. commissioned Ruben's to paint the ceiling of the main hall. Fourteen years later on January 30th. 1649, King Charles 1 st. stepped out of a first floor window onto a scaffold and was beheaded.
Open 10.a.m. to 5.0 pm.

King Charles 1st. Bust and plaque - The Banqueting House entrance.

On the corner here at Horse Guards Avenue is a statue to the 8th. Duke of Devonshire

- Spencer Compton KG Born 1833. died 1908. The family own the magnificent Chatsworth House and estate in Derbyshire. Another plaque to a later member of the family - Lord Frederick Cavendish, who was murdered in Dublin, can be see in St. Margaret's Church, near the end of the walk. See my book - "Famous Derbyshire People - The Earls and Dukes of Devonshire", for more information on this leading family.

Opposite is the Queen's Life Guards and the changing of the Horse Guards takes place during the week at 11.0 a.m. and at 10.0 a.m. on Sundays.

Pass the Old War Office on the right and in the middle of the road, a monument to -

Field Marshall His Royal Highness George, Duke o Cambridge KG GCB etc.

Ahead can be seen Nelson's Monument and Trafalgar Square. Turn right along Whitehall Place. on your left at No. 3/8 -

Site of Scotland Yard.
First Headquarters of the Metropolitan Police - 1829-1890.
The actual Scotland Yard is at the rear.

Pass the DEFRA offices and at the junction with Whitehall Court on the right is -

Royal Tank Regiment Memorial Statue; opened by the Queen - Colonel in Chief - on 13th. June 2000.
The memorial shows the five man crew of a World War 2 Comet Tank in 1945.
The crew of five consisted of - Commander, Gunner, Loader, Hull Machine Gun Gunner and Driver.
One of the most successful tanks with a 77 m.m. High Velocity gun and powered by a 600 h.p. Rolls Royce engine.

Continue along Whitehall Place to Northumberland Avenue and Embankment. Turn right and left to cross the Golden Jubilee Bridge over the River Thames. On your right is the Hispaniola boat and Victoria Embankment Gardens, which has numerous statues and memorials. Part way across stop and admire the view to the London Eye and Houses of Parliament. Turn right at the end and descend to the Thames Path and Jubilee Gardens. On your left is the Shell Centre built 1957-62. Pass a flag pole on your left -

Presented by the Forestry Industry of British Columbia, Canada for the 1951 Festival of Britain. Re-erected here in 1977 to mark the Silver Jubilee of Queen Elizabeth 2nd.

Just after is the Jubilee Oracle sculpture by Alexander, 1980. Pass the London Eye (2000) and then the former County Hall and Dali Exhibition and the London Aquarium before Westminster Bridge - built 1854-62 and designed by Thomas Page. To your left is the Florence Nightingale Museum - open every day. Turn left then right into Lambeth Palace Road.

Florence Nightingale, "The lady with lamp". Born in Florence and brought up in Derbyshire. She went to the Crimean War and revolutionised nursing. See my book - "Famous Derbyshire People - Florence Nightingale", for more information on her life.

Keep straight ahead, still on the Thames Path and pass St. Thomas Hospital on your left. The new part dates from 1969/75 and older part - 1865. From the path you have good views of the Houses of Parliament opposite.

Lambeth Palace Gatehouse. The Museum of Garden History is on the right.

Continue to Lambeth Bridge, with Lambeth Palace and the Museum of Garden History on your left. The entrance is through a former church. Near the porch entrance on the right can be seen the tomb -

Family tomb of John Field, Wax Chandler of this parish 1742 - 1790.

Just inside the porch is -

In Memory of William Bacon
of the Salt Office, London,
Gent. who was killed by
thunder and lightning at this window
July 12th. 1787
Aged 34 years

Turn right across Lambeth Bridge and right at the end and descend steps to the Victoria Tower Gardens. The Houses of Parliament are ahead, with the Victoria Tower built in 1860. A short distance in the park is the Slave Well -

"This plaque Commemorates the 150th. Anniversary of the antislavery Society - 1839 - 1989."

Turn left at the well to the main road, Abingdon Street , and cross over into Dean Stanley Street to St. John's Concert Hall. Bear right and right along Lord North Street. At house No. 5 -

W. T. Stead 1849 - 1912
Journalist and reformer
of great renown,
lived here 1904 - 1912.

Cross the next road into Cowley Street and pass No. 4 as you turn left - the Liberal Democrats Headquarters. House No 6 -

Lord Reith 1889 - 1971
- Director General of
the B.B.C.,
lived here 1924 - 1930.

Follow the road right, now Barton Street. and on the right side of house No. 7 can be seen the words and arrow -

"Public shelters in vault under pavements in the street."

House No. 14 -

T. E. Lawrence -
"Lawrence of Arabia"
lived here 1888 - 1935.

Just after turn left along Great College Street and in a short distance where it turns left - Tufton Street, turn right through the doorway into Westminster School. (If the doorway is closed turn left then right along Little Smith Street to Great Smith Street. Turn right along it to Victoria Street and Westminster Abbey). Walk through the quadrangle aiming for the top lefthand corner and gateway. Through and on the right is Westminster Abbey.

Wetsminster Abbey and St. Margaret's church, in front.

WESTMINSTER ABBEY - *Every English King and Queen since Edward the Confessor, have been crowned here - the Coronation Chair is here - and most buried here, including the tragic, Mary Queen of Scots . Many leading people have memorials, including Issac Newton, Darwin, Handel and Purcell. A walk around will bring you to Henry VII chapel, Poet's Corner, Chapter House and cloisters. The building is a mixture of styles but is predominately 13th. century, Early English Gothic. The building is administered by the Crown and has never been made a cathedral.*

ST. MARGARET'S CHURCH - *Stands infront of Westminster Abbey - full of history and monuments - well worth a visit.*

Turn right past the Abbey and church to Parliament Square.

Around the square are statue monuments to Abraham Lincoln, George Canning, Viscount Palmerston, Ian Christian Smith, Sir Winston Churchill, Beaconsfield, and Peel - 1788 - 1850.

Sir Winston Churchill Statue - Parliament Square.

Keep right then left past the square with the Houses of Parliament on the right, to Bridge Street where you began.

THE PALACE OF WESTMINSTER - ***Built in neo-Gothic style in 1840. The Victoria Tower dates from 1860. Home to both Houses of Parliament and when in session visitor's are allowed to the House of Commons and House of Lords Visitor's Galleries', free. To your right is Big Ben - The bell you hear today is the second bell to placed here in 1856.***

Cross to your right back to the Westminster Underground Station.

MONKS, MURDER, PUNISHMENT, & POETRY - Map One

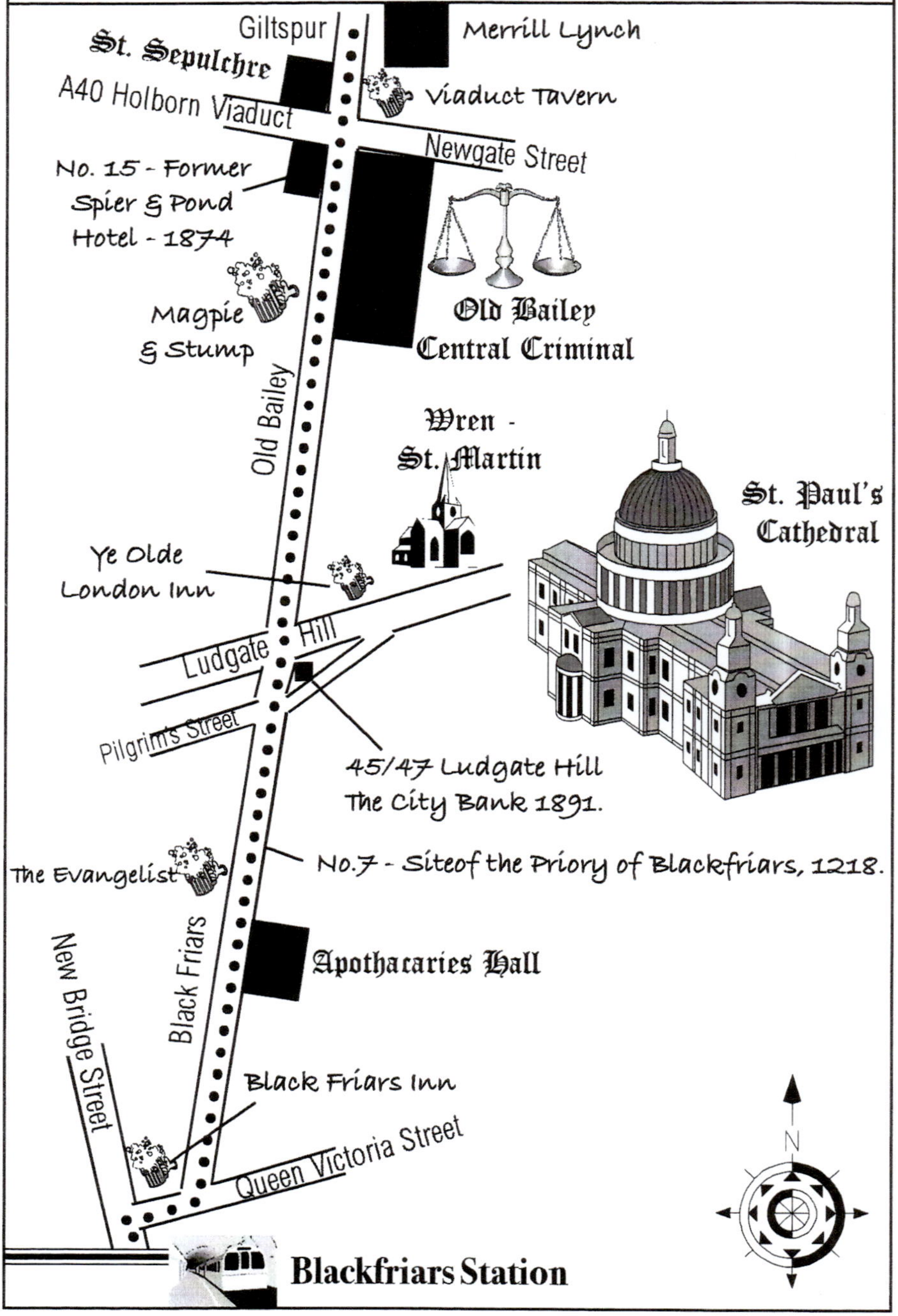

MONKS, MURDER, PUNISHMENT & POETRY

1 1/2 miles - allow 3 hours

Basic route - Blackfriars Underground Station - Black Friars Lane - Ludgate Hill - Old Bailey - Giltspur - Smithfield Market - Cloth Court - Middle Street - Aldersgate - Barbican Underground Station.

Start - Blackfriars Underground Station - Circle Line.
End - Barbican Underground Station - Circle Line.

Inns - Numerous on the walk, including - Black Friars inn, The Evangelist, Ye Olde London Inn, Magpie & Stump, Viaduct Tavern, The Butchers Hook and Cleaver, The Rising Sun and Old Red Cow.

Coffee - several along the route.

ABOUT THE WALK - A veritable mix of fascinating places to see and visit along this short walk - allow a good three hours or more to visit the churches and museums along the way. You will see where monks built their Church's and Priory's; where many a renowned murder trial took place; an area where body snatching was prevalent in the 18th. century; the scene for many an unlawful and horrific murder; where wife's were brought to be sold at market and the former home of a poet laureate. Interspersed are historical plaques, and fascinating church's - some of the finest in the land - and St. Bartholomew's Museum to explore and perhaps a visit to the spectator's gallery in the Old Bailey!

WALKING INSTRUCTIONS - Exit Blackfriars Station following signs for Blackfriars Bridge/Millennium Bridge. Gaining the road, turn right and follow it right - Queen Victoria Street - with the Black Friars Inn opposite. Cross the road and turn left towards the inn and before it right along Black Friars Lane - path signed St. Paul's. First pass The Apothecaries Hall on your right, then

Black Friars Inn.

the Evangelist on the left before reaching No. 7 on the right - a plaque here records the ***"Site of the Priory of Blackfriars, 1278."***

Apothecaries Hall coat of arms.

Just after keep straight ahead across Pilgrims Street to Ludgate Hill. On the right is No. 45-47 Ludgate Hill, formerly The City Bank, 1891. Cross the road into Old Bailey. To your right is St. Martins, Wren church - well worth a visit - and St. Paul's Cathedral, which is part of, the Great Fire 1666 Walk - next walk!

Continue along Old Bailey and pass the Central Criminal Court on your right - The public gallery is open daily, see times on the noticeboard. Pass the Magpie and Stump on the left and reach Holborn Viaduct, with No 15 on the left, formerly the Spier and Pond Hotel, 1874. Go straight across into Giltspur with the Viaduct Tavern on the righthand corner. On your left is the church of the Holy Sepulchre.

The Old Bailey and the Scales of Justice.

HOLY SEPULCHRE - *Known at St Sepulchre without Newgate, the site was originally of a Saxon church dedicated to St. Edmund. This was rebuilt in 1450 of which the present tower, walls and porch remain. During the Great Fire of London in 1666, the church was badly damaged but was restored in 1670. Since then it has undergone much alteration. As the history board outside the porch recalls, many famous people have been associated with the church over the centuries, these include -*

John Rogers, Vicar, the first Protestant Martyr.
Roger Aschan, tutor to Queen Elizabeth 1st.
William Harvey, the discoverer of the circulation of blood.
Sir Henry Wood, famous for the annual Promenade Concerts and whose ashes are now in the Musicians chapel.
The 8th. Battalion of the Royal Fusiliers (The City of London Regiment) has a chapel here and remembrance garden.

Finally the church bells are the "Bells of Old Bailey" in the nursery rhyme - "Oranges and Lemons."

On the lefthand corner of Giltspur is a small drinking fountain complete with chained cups - ***"On Holborn Hill in 1859. Here is 1867. Gift of Samuel Gurney M.P. 1859."***

MONKS, MURDER, PUNISHMENT, & POETRY - Map Two

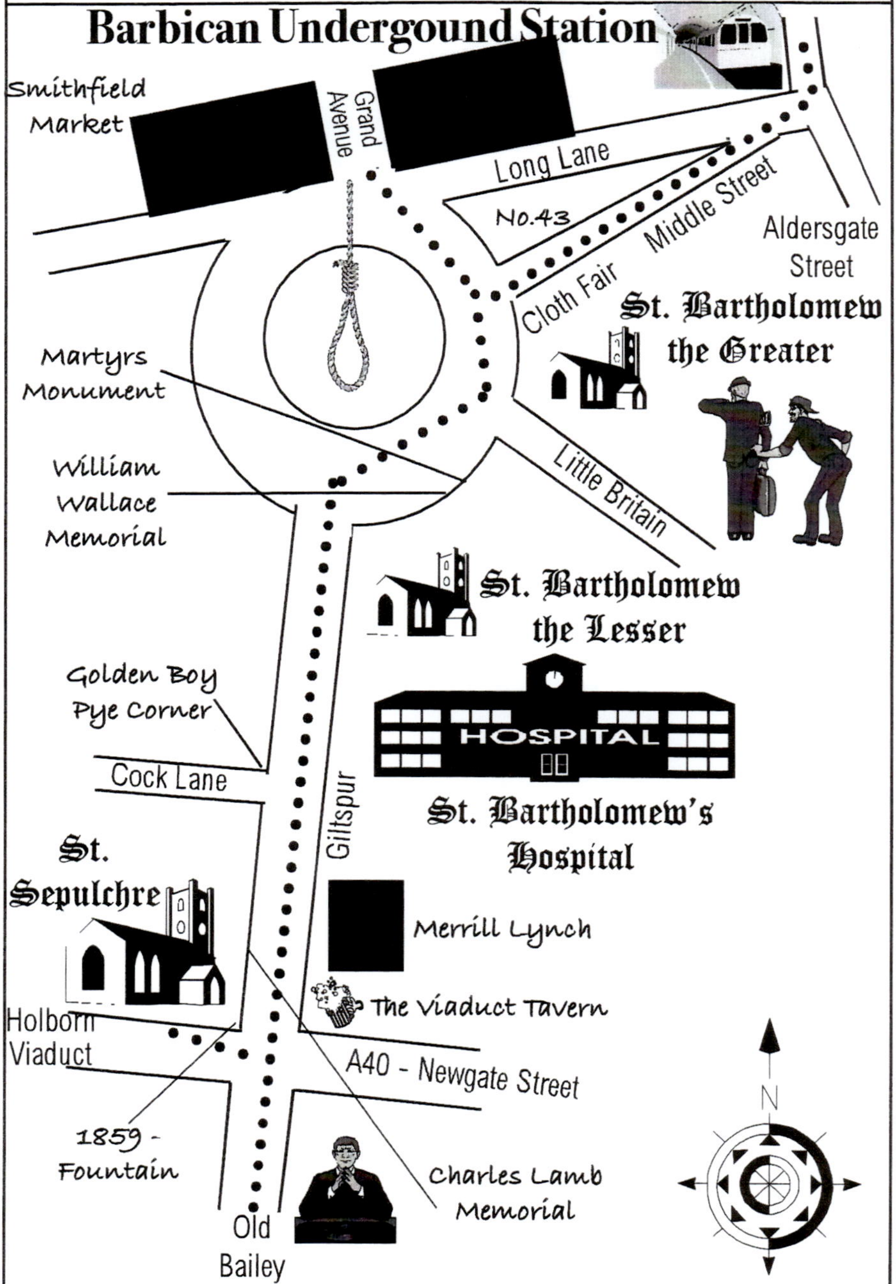

Walk along Giltspur with Merrill Lynch on the right - no relation! In a few yards on the left wall of the church is a monument to Charles Lamb.

"The Memorial was moved here in December 1962 from Christchurch Greyfrairs in Newgate Street. Which stands beside the former site of Charles Lamb school Christ's Hospital."

"Charles lamb - Perhaps the most loved name in English Literature who was a Bluecoat Boy here 7 years. B. 1775. d. 1834."

On the immediate right is the Watch House, erected 1791, and part of the church, o keep an eye on the churchyard for the body snatchers. Destroyed 1941. Rebuilt 1962.

Continue along Giltspur with St. Bartholomew's Hospital on the right. On the left on the corner of Cock Lane is the Golden Boy at Pye Corner.

A memorial to the Great Fire of London ion 1666 and to body snatchers. There 18th. century work meant digging up newly buried bodies from the churchyard and giving them to the surgeons to practise on!

THE GOLDEN BOY OF PYE CORNER

THE BOY AT PYE CORNER WAS ERECTED TO COMMEMORATE THE STAYING OF THE GREAT FIRE WHICH BEGINNING AT PUDDING LANE WAS ASCRIBED TO THE SIN OF GLUTTONY WHEN NOT ATTRIBUTED TO THE PAPISTS AS ON THE MONUMENT AND THE BOY WAS MADE PRODIGIOUSLY FAT TO ENFORCE THE MORAL HE WAS ORIGINALLY BUILT INTO THE FRONT OF A PUBLIC HOUSE CALLED FORTUNE OF WAR WHICH USED TO OCCUPY THIS SITE AND WAS PULLED DOWN IN 1910

THE FORTUNE OF WAR WAS THE CHIEF HOUSE OF CALL NORTH OF THE RIVER FOR RESURRECTIONISTS IN BODY SNATCHING DAYS YEARS AGO THE LANDLORD USED TO SHOW THE ROOM WHERE ON BENCHES ROUND THE WALLS THE BODIES WERE PLACED LABELLED WITH THE SNATCHERS NAMES WAITING TILL THE SURGEONS AT SAINT BARTHOLOMEW'S COULD RUN ROUND AND APPRAISE THEM.

A little further on the right is the entrance to the Hospital's Museum and almost immediately on your left is the church of St. Bartholomew the Less. Both worth a visit.

Continue along the righthand side of the road and pass the monument to William Wallace; the monument speaks for itself.

Just after is another monument -

"The Noble Army of Martyr Praise Thee.
Within a few feet of this spot
John Rogers (Vicar of St. Sepulchre)
John Bradford
John Philpot
and others
Servants of God
Suffered death by fire
for the faith of Christ
in the year 1555, 1556, 1557."

Just after is the 13th. century gate house of the Priory Church of St. Bartholomew The Great.

Gatehouse and entry
to the Priory Church of St. Bartholomew the Greater.

The Prior Rohere tomb.

PRIORY CHURCH OF ST. BARTHOLOMEW THE GREAT - ***One of the most interesting churches in London. Founded in 1123 by Prior Rahere, who also founded the hospital, died in 1143. His tomb is on the left of the High Altar. The dark interior of the church has splendid Norman columns and numerous memorials. The entrance gate is the most impressive gateway to a church in London.***

Your route is now right along Cloth Fair, but first bear left to visit the Grand Avenue of Smithfield Market.

In time past the area was renowned for muggers and pickpockets and had the reputation of being one of "the roughest places in London." The locals had a distinct dislike for outsiders and with a history of burning at the stake and lynching, as we have seen on the plaques, it was no wonder it was notorious.

WIFE SELLING - ***In the 19th century divorce was almost impossible to obtain and a way round it was to bring your wife to market, with a halter around here neck, and try to sell her! Often they were sold sold for 2 shillings and six pence (12 1/2p), which the husband then spent on drink! - an example of 1833, at Epping Market. A poem was published on 12th. august 1811 about the wife selling antics of John Hobbs, which includes this verse -***

He tried to sell her but couldn't and eventually they left, "Happy ever after!"

> ***"Oh, who'll buy a wife? says John Hobbs, John Hobbs***
> ***A sweet pretty wife, says Hobbs,***
> ***But somehow they tell us,***
> ***The wife-dealing fellows,***
> ***Were all of of them sellers***
> ***John Hobbs, John Hobbs***
> ***And none of 'em wanted Jane Hobbs!"***

Return past the Butchers Hook and Cleaver Inn and on along Cloth Fair. At No 43, cloth Court, on the left is a plaque to Sir John Betjeman - probably Britain's finest 20th. century poet and a former Poet Laureate.

The Last Laugh by John Betjeman

I made hay while the sun shone.
My work sold.
Now, if the harvest is over
And the world cold,
Give me the bonus of laughter
As I lose hold.

Continue along the Cloth Fair and on straight ahead along Middle Street, passing the Rising Sun Inn and Old Red Cow. On the right pass the Founders Hall. Reach Long Lane and turn right to Aldersgate Street. Turn left and in a few yards reach the Barbican Underground Station.

THE GREAT FIRE OF LONDON - 1666 - 5 MILES - *Map One*

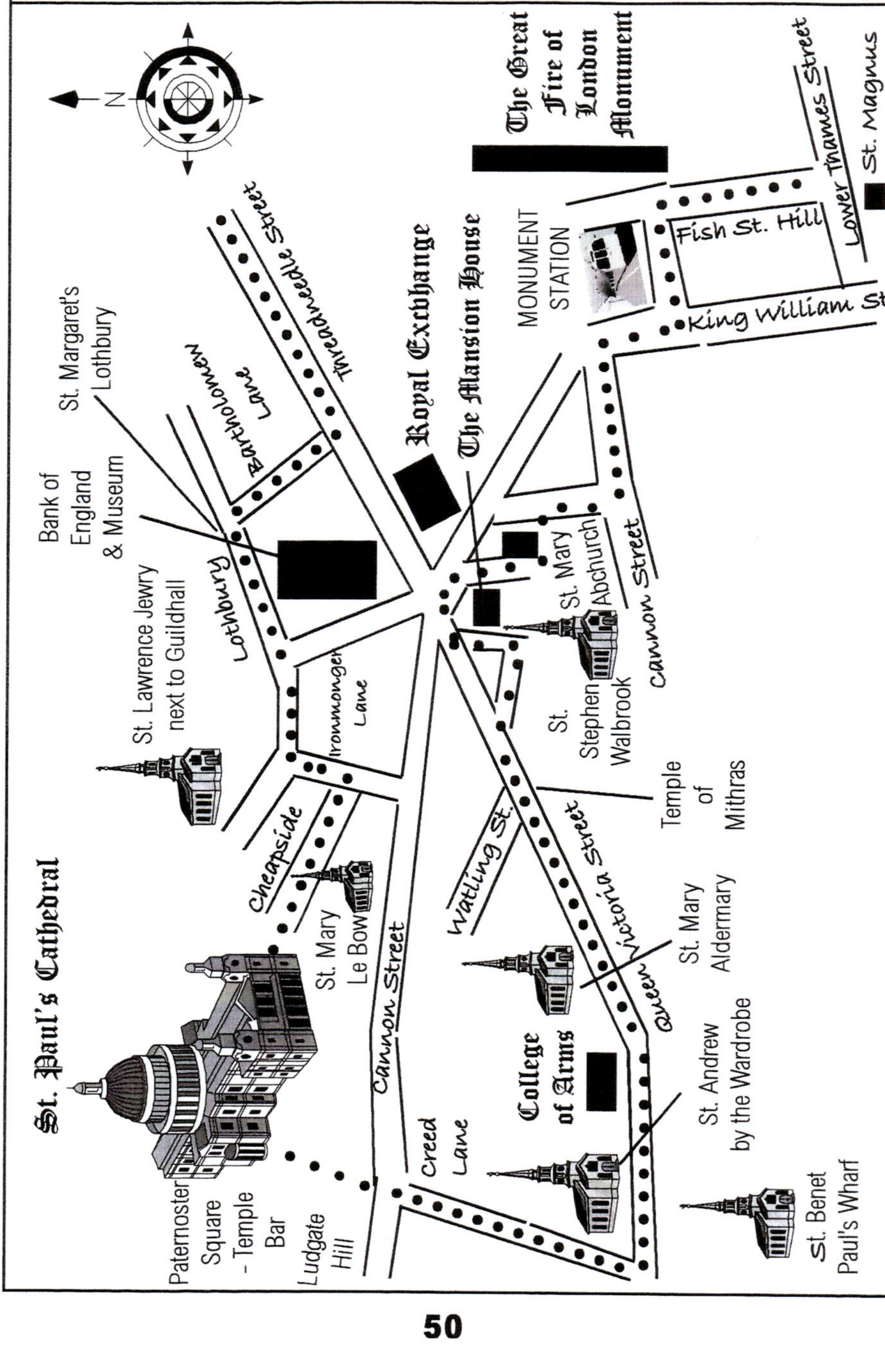

THE GREAT FIRE OF LONDON - 1666
- 5 miles
- allow 5 hours

***Basic route** - Monument Underground Station - The Monument - St. Mary Abchurch - St. Mary of Woolnoth - Mansion House - St. Stephen of Walbrook - Temple of Mithras - Cole Abbey - College of Arms - Guild Church of St. Benet - St. Andrew by the Wardrobe - St. Paul's Cathedral - Temple Bar - St. Vedast -St. Mary le Bow - St. Lawrence Jewry, next to Guildhall - St. Margaret's, Lothbury - Bank of England - Royal Exchange - Threadneedle Street - St. Helen's - St. Andrew Undershaft Church - St. Catherine Cree Church - St. Botolph's, Aldgate - St. Olaves Church - All Hallows by the Tower - Tower of London - Thames Path - St. Magnus the Martyr - Monument Underground Station.*

***Start and end** - Monument Underground Station (Circle & District Line).*
Since you pass several other underground stations you can stop where you want, such as Tower Hill on the District & Circle lines.

***Inns** - you pass many along the way, especially The Cockpit Inn on Bgon Street Hill, before St. Paul's Cathedral.*

***Cafe's** - Numerous along the whole way.*

ABOUT THE WALK - The main aim of the walk is to see the churches rebuilt by Sir Christopher Wren, following the Great Fire of London in 1666. You see more than twelve of them; one that escaped the fire and another, the oldest church in the City of London and where Samuel Pepys watched the fire. You see the small churches of Wren's work and his finest achievement - St. Paul's Cathedral. But as you walk along you also see considerable history dating back to Roman times and can visit the Tower of London. But first you start with a climb - The Monument - it is best to do it at the start when you are fresh, as well as seeing from above many of the places you will be visiting; on your descent you receive a certificate! There is a plethora of places to visit on this walk so don't feel obliged to visit everything - come back another day and see the places you omitted.

THE MONUMENT - ***Standing 202 feet (62m) from the Bakers shop in Pudding Lane, where the Great Fire of 1666 started, the Monument - the tallest free standing Doric column in the world, made from Portland Stone, is exactly 202 feet high (62m). Built to commemorate the Great Fire between 1671-77 by Sir Christopher Wren and Dr. Robert Hooke. To reach the balcony at 160 feet (50m.) you ascend 311 steps.***

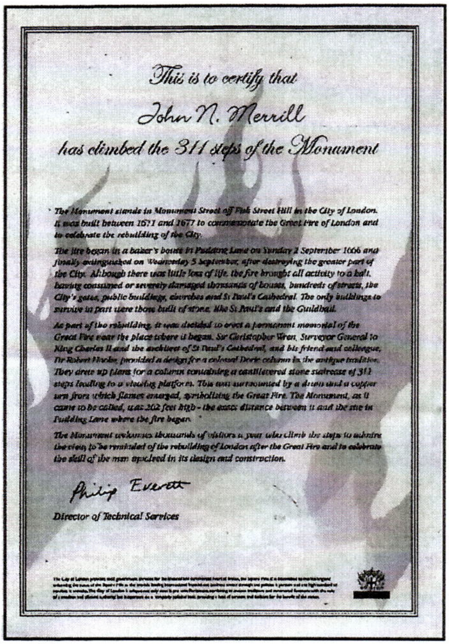

This is to certify that

John N. Merrill

has climbed the 311 steps of the Monument

The Monument stands in Monument Street off Fish Street Hill in the City of London. It was built between 1671 and 1677 to commemorate the Great Fire of London and to celebrate the rebuilding of the City.

The fire began in a baker's house in Pudding Lane on Sunday 2 September 1666 and finally extinguished on Wednesday 5 September, after destroying the greater part of the City. Although there was little loss of life, the fire brought all activity to a halt, having consumed or severely damaged thousands of houses, hundreds of streets, the City's gates, public buildings, churches and St Paul's Cathedral. The only buildings to survive in part were those built of stone, like St Paul's and the Guildhall.

As part of the rebuilding, it was decided to erect a permanent memorial of the Great Fire near the place where it began. Sir Christopher Wren, Surveyor General to King Charles II and the architect of St Paul's Cathedral, and his friend and colleague, Dr Robert Hooke, provided a design for a colossal Doric column in the antique tradition. They drew up plans for a column containing a cantilevered stone staircase of 311 steps leading to a viewing platform. This was surmounted by a drum and a copper urn from which flames emerged, symbolising the Great Fire. The Monument, as it came to be called, was 202 feet high - the exact distance between it and the site in Pudding Lane where the fire began.

The Monument welcomes thousands of visitors a year who climb the steps to admire the view, to be reminded of the rebuilding of London after the Great Fire and to celebrate the skill of the men involved in its design and construction.

Philip Everett

Director of Technical Services

My certificate!

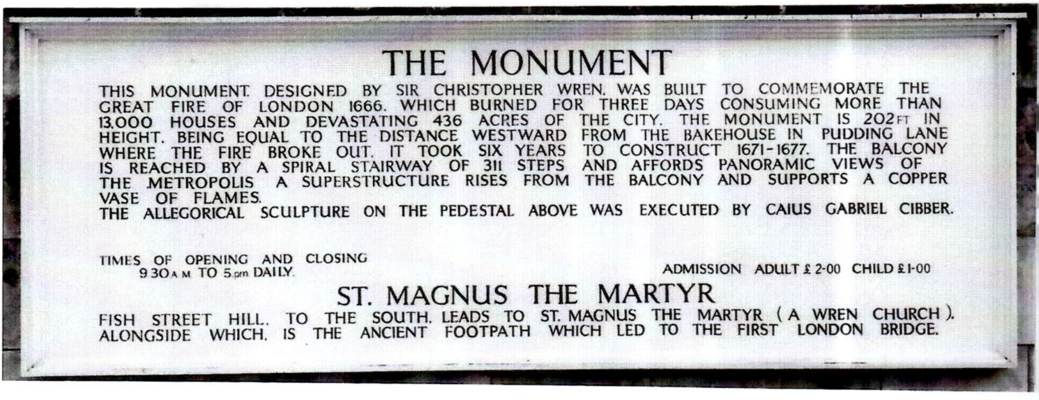

The Monument.

The Great Fire, started on September 2nd. 1666 in a bakers shop in Pudding Lane, and burnt for four days, destroying 472 acres, 51 churches and 13,000 buildings - about 80% of London. - but only eight people died. The Lord Mayor went to bed the first night dismissing the fire as, "something a woman might pisse out!" But with wind the fire spread rapidly. The architect, Sir Christopher Wren was given the task of rebuilding the city, and although his overhall plan was not taken up, he rebuilt the churches and created the masterpiece - St. Paul's cathedral, which reopened in 1710.

Monument views - to River Thames, Tower Bridge and City Hall.

Monument views - to St. Paul's Cathedral.

Monument views - to the Financial District - Lloyds, Gherkin and Tower 42.

Monument views - to St. Magnus Church and south bank of the Rirver Thames.

WALKING INSTRUCTIONS - Exit the Monument underground station at Fish Street Hill and turn right for The Monument - open 9.30 a.m. to 5.0. p.m. daily. At the bottom of Fish Street Hill is St. Magnus the Martyr church - rebuilt by Wren and your return route. To your right is Canon Street, your route, but first The Monument. Ascend the 311 steps to the balcony and see the dome of St. Paul's Cathedral, many church spires and Tower Bridge - all of your route! Descend and receive your certificate and return to Fish Street Hill. Keep straight ahead along Canon Street and turn right along Abchurch Lane to St. Mary Abchurch on the left. Turn left to the church and keep left around it and keep left to walk along Sherborne Lane to King William Street and St. Mary Woolnoth.

ST. MARY WOOLNOTH - ***Designed by Nicholas Hawksmoor, Sir Christopher Wren's assistant. It is the only church he designed in the city and he is more famous for Christchurch, Spitalfields. The outside has twin towers and inside Corinthian columns.***

Keep left along King William Street to the road junction with the Royal Exchange and Bank of England on the right and beside you on the left the Mansion House - the residence of the Lord Mayor of the City of London.

THE MANSION HOUSE - ***Every November, as originated in the Magna Carter of 1215, the newly appointed Mayor goes in a state coach to the Royal Courts of Justice for their approval. The event now known as The Lord Mayors Show, is accompanied by floats and a fireworks display. The porticoed Mansion House was built in the 18th. century by George Dance the Elder - City Surveyor. The area close to the Mansion House is where the Stocks Market was held between 1282 - 1737.***

The Royal Exchange.

Immediately at the side of the Mansion House turn left by the City of London Magistrates Court to St. Stephen Walbrook church.

ST. STEPHEN WALBROOK CHURCH - ***An impressive Wren city church built in 1679; many consider it to be his finest church and a glimpse of his ideas for St. Paul's Cathedral, with 16 Corinthian capitals supporting a dome.***

Turn right opposite the church along Bucklersbury to Queen Victoria Street. Turn left and on the right are the ruins of the Roman Temple of Mithras dating back to the 3rd. century. Opposite is the Roman Road - Watling Street.

Continue along Queen Victoria Street, which now keep on for the next 1/2 mile. Pass on your right the Guild Church of St. Mary , Aldermary.

THE GUILD CHURCH OF ST. MARY, ALDER MARY - ***Rebuilt by Wren's office, after the fire, between 1679 - 82. The interior is particularly notable for its fine fan vaulted ceilings.***

Next pass the Cole Abbey Presbyterian church on the right and then also on the right is the College of Arms.

COLLEGE OF ARMS - *Open Monday to Friday - 10.0 .a.m. to 4.0 p.m. The original building was destroyed by the fire and the present buildings dates from the 1670's. Well worth a visit and the place to see Heraldry and trace your family history*.

Almost opposite on the left, down steps, is ***The Guild Church of St. Benet, Paul's Wharf - a Welsh church.***

Continue along Queen Victoria Street and pass the Faraday Building on the right - ***"Site of Doctors Commons; demolished 1867"*** - to the next church on the right, St. Andrew by the Wardrobe.

ST. ANDREW BY THE WARDROBE - ***Wren city church which was badly hit during the blitz in World War Two, but since fully restored. Gets its name from the fact that the King's wardrobe - furniture and armour - was moved here from the Tower of London, to just north of the church, during medieval times. Destroyed by the great fire. Inside in the west gallery is a memorial to William Shakespeare who worked for fifteen years nearby at Blackfriars Theatre, and lived in the parish for a while.***

Turn right beside the church along St. Andrew's Hill. Keep ahead and pass The Cockpit Inn and cross Carter Lane, to continue along Creed Lane to Ludgate Hill. Turn right to St. Paul's Cathedral.

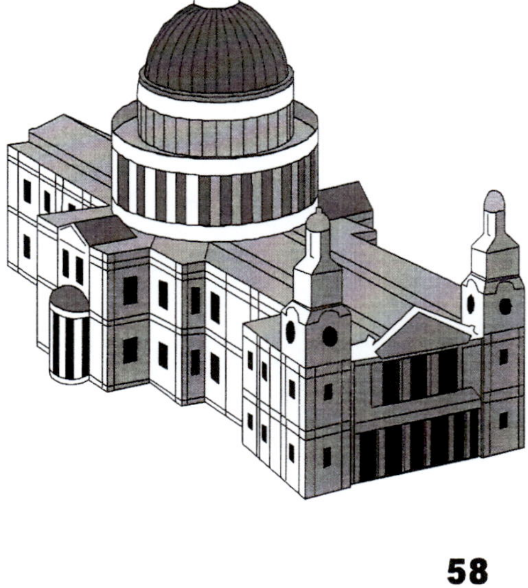

ST. PAUL'S CATHEDRAL - ***Wren's masterpiece with one of the largest free standing domes in the world. The first service was held here in 1697 and since then has been a major focal point weddings and funerals through the centuries. Inside there is much to see, notably the dome and the Whispering Gallery; St. Dunstan's Chapel, the crypt, choir stalls and the tombs of Wren, Nelson and Wellington. Open daily. Limited free access on a Sunday.***

The Dome of St. Paul's Cathedral.

Keep to the lefthand side of the cathedral - St. Paul's churchyard. On your left at the start is Paternoster Square, Temple Bar and another Great Fire monument.

TEMPLE BAR - ***The only surviving gateway into the City of London. Originally built in the city in 1672, but became "redundant" until it was bought by the wealthy brewer, Sir Henry Meux, for his grounds at Theobalds Park , Cheshunt, Hertfordshire. There it remained for more than century and a local inn is still called, Temple Bar. A trust was established and raised the money to have it returned and rebuilt here in November 2004.***

Continue along St. Paul's Churchyard to Cheapside. To your left is St. Vedast - alias Foster church. Continue along Cheapside to your next church on your right - St. Mary le Bow.

ST. MARY LE BOW - ***Built by Wren in 1673 and the steeple is considered one of his best works. The church bells are famous; if you were born within the sounds of the bells, you are a cockney.***

The Temple Bar with Patnernoster Square beyond.

Continue a little further along Cheapside and pass Barclays bank on the left and immediately after turn left into Ironmonger Lane. Just before you do is a plaque recording that Thomas a Beckett as born here; he later became Archbishop of Canterbury and subsequently murdered in the cathedral - a martyr and saint.

Pass St. Olaves House in Ironmonger Lane and reach Gresham Street/Lothbury Road. To your left is St. Lawrence Jewry, next to Guildhall and The Guildhall.

St. Lawrence Jewry next to the Guildhall.

ST. LAWRENCE JEWRY NEXT TO GUILDHALL - ***The original 12th. century church built in 1136 was in the Jewish quarter, hence its name today. The building was destroyed by the great fire and the Wren church was completed in 1680. During World War Two it was destroyed but by 1957 was completely restored and is now the Church of the Corporation of London. Samuel Pepys wrote - "Well pleased with the church, it being a very free church."***

The Guildhall.

GUILDHALL - ***Much of the present building is 15th. century but parts were destroyed during the great fire and blitz. Situated in the Square Mile, it is the City of London's administration offices, where for the last 800 years, has governed the city.***

Turn right along Gresham Street and on along Lothbury, to pass on your left, St. Margaret's Lothbury.

On you right is the Bank of England. Turn right down its side along Bartholomew Lane, and in doing so pass the entrance to the Bank of England Museum - admission free and well worth a visit.

THE GREAT FIRE OF LONDON - 1666 - 5 MILES - *Map Two*

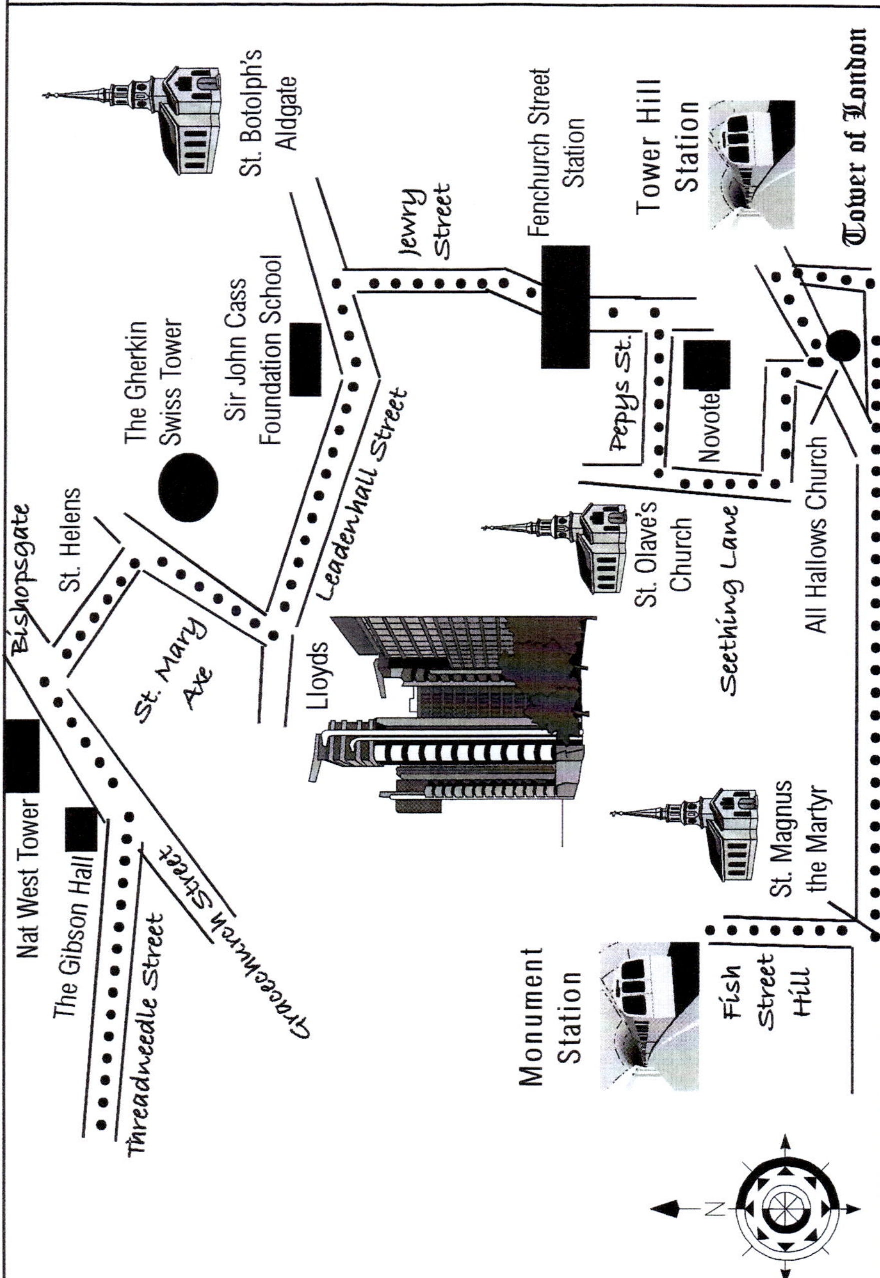

Reach Threadneedle Street and turn left with the Royal Exchange opposite. Continue along Threadneedle Street to its junction with Gracechurch Street/ Bishopgate with The Gibson Hall on the lefthand corner. Turn left along Bishopsgate and in a few yards opposite the Nat west Bank Tower No. 42, turn right along Great St. Helens. You are now in the financial district of the city. Reach St. Helens church on the left.

Continue ahead a little further to the skyscraper - Swiss Re Tower - affectionately known as, The Gherkin. The round glass tower has 41 storeys and is a distinct building on London's skyline. Turn right along St. Mary's Axe to St. Andrew's Undershaft Church

Church & The Swiss Re Tower (Gherkin).

The tower is 540 fet high; has 744 windows and 24,000 square metres of glass.

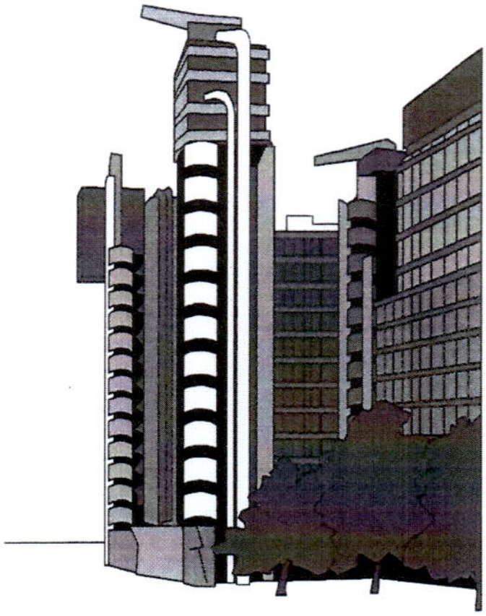

Turn left along Leadenhall Street with the Steel complex of Lloyds Building opposite. Soon pass on your left, St. Katherine Cree Church

ST. CATHERINE CREE CHURCH - ***Built in 1628 and one of only eight churches in the city to survive the great fire. The word Cree reminds us that this was once the Priory of Christ Church founded in 1108. The church was built for the public so that the m monks could continue their worship in the peace and quiet of the priory.***

Continue along the rest of Leadenhall Street to its junction with Aldgate. On the left is St. John Cass's Foundation Primary School, founded in 1710. Turn left and before turning right down Jewry Street, just ahead is St. Botolph's, Aldgate.

Walk down Jewry Street and pass the Crutched Friars on the right. At the end bear part left to walk along Coopers Row underneath Fenchurch Street Station. Just after at the Novotel Hotel, turn right along Pepys Street. Pass Pepys Bar and at the end reach Seething Lane and St. Olaves Church.

ST. OLAVE'S CHURCH - ***St. Olav is the patron saint of Norway, with the cathedral of Trondheim being the principal church. It is the only St. Olav church in the city and was founded in the 11th. century. The crypt chapel dates from the 13th. century and the tower is 15th. century. The burial register has several interesting entries including -***

> ***1586. September 14th. Mother Goose.***
> ***1665 - the Great Plague; 365 names.***
> ***1703. June 4th. Samuel Pepys. Lies buried in the vault under the communion table.***

Turn left along Seething Lane and left along Muscovy Street to Trinity Square and Tower Hill Underground Station. Turn right to Byward Street and to your right is All Hallows by the Tower church.

ALL HALLOWS BY THE TOWER CHURCH - ***The oldest church in the City of London - a church has been on this site over 1300 years. From the tower, Samuel Pepys watched the great fire. Much of the building was destroyed during World War Two and subsequently rebuilt. The church has a strong American connection with William Penn being baptised here and John Quincy Adams, who became the USA 6th. President, married here.***

Turn left towards the Tower of London and large war memorial and Trinity Square Gardens on your left. Just beyond them is the best piece of the Roman wall that surrounded the city in Roman times; infront is a statue of the Roman Emperor, Trajan - 98 - 117 AD. - ***Photo opposite*** Retrace your steps and turn left down to the shop, ticket office and entrance to the Tower of London.

THE TOWER OF LONDON - ***London's and England's most visited building. Here for over 900 years much of the history of England has been witnessed. Founded by William the Conqueror it houses the Crown Jewels, famed for the Yeoman Warders (Beefeaters), where Anne Boleyn was executed, where Guy Fawkes was interrogated, and where many traitors were imprisoned over the centuries in the Bloody Tower.***

Beefeaters at the entrance to the Tower of London.

The Tower of London and Traitor's Gate on the left.

Turn right onto the Thames path and follow it for more than 1/4 mile with the river on your left and the Custom House on your right. Just before London Bridge turn right to reach St. Magnus the Martyr church, which you saw at the start.

ST. MAGNUS THE MARTYR CHURCH - ***Your last church, but one of considerable interest. Beside the porch is a small piece of wood which is believed to have come from the Roman Wharf here in AD 75 and found in Fish Street Hill in 1991. Inside the church can be seen a replica of the original London Bridge, which for 700 years acted as a major crossing the river. The church is dedicated to St. Magnus, Earl of Orkney in the 11th. century, he was later murdered in the early 12th. century. The church was among the first to be lost to the great fire and Samuel Pepys in his diary wrote of September 2nd. 1666 - "It hath burned down St. Magnus church and most of Fish street already." Another church, St. Margaret New Fish Street, was also burned down and is where the Monument was built, as St. Magnus church was the main one. Wren's craftsmen were busy here and by 1676 much of the work had been done. The steeple was not completed until 1706. The interior has many interesting monuments including Miles Coverdale, who later became Bishop of Exeter and oversaw the printing of the Bible in English in 1535.***

Plaque in the side of St. Magnus Church.

Cross the Lower Thames Road into Fish Street Hill and pass The Monument where you began, back to the The Monument Underground Station.

Plaque on Fish Street Hill.

BRIDGES, BOATS & DUNGEONS - 3 MILES

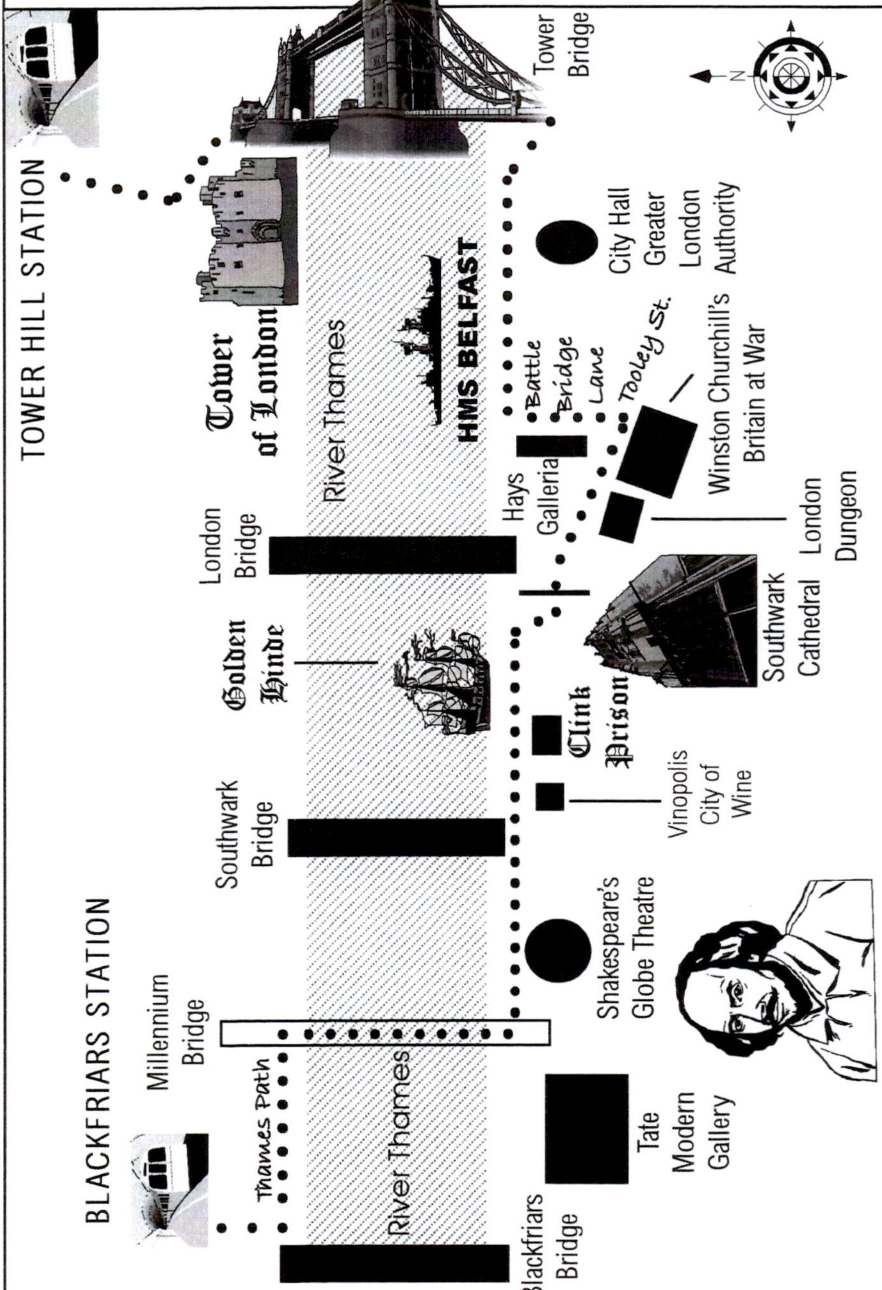

BRIDGES, BOATS AND DUNGEONS - 3 MILES - allow 2 to 3 hours.

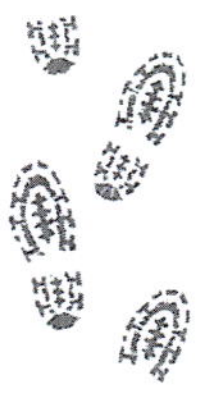

***Basic route** - Tower Hill Underground Station - Tower of London - Tower Bridge - Thames Path - HMS Belfast - Hays Galleria - Winston Churchill's Britain at War - London Dungeon - Southwark Cathedral - Golden Hinde - Clink Prison - Southwark Bridge - Shakespeare's Globe Theatre - Millennium Bridge - Thames Path - Blackfriars Underground Station.*

***Start** - Tower Hill Underground Station - Circle & District Line.*
***End** - Blackfriars Underground Station - Circle & District Line.*

***Inns** - Shipwright Arms, Tooley Street. The Barrowboy and Banker, Brough High Street. Old Thameside Inn, near Golden Hinde. Vinopollis, City of Wine. The Anchor near Southwark Bridge.*

***Cafe's and restaurant's** - numerous - in Hays Galleria. Bankside near Southwark Bridge area.*

ABOUT THE WALK - A morning stroll along the south bank of the Thames, crossing the spectacular Tower Bridge and ultramodern Millennium bridge from Shakespeare's Globe Theatre to St. Paul's. In-between is a huge wealth of interest - the ships Golden Hinde and HMS Belfast; the London Dungeon Museum and Clink Prison Museum; Winston Churchill's Battle of Britain Exhibition; Shopping in Hays Galleria; Southwark Cathedral and the Shakespeare's Globe Theatre. As with all these walks you can pick and choose what you want to explore/visit further as you pass by. From the bridges you have fine views over the city, picking out many of the well known landmarks. You start at the Tower of London and if you haven't visited this on another walk, then you can visit this first.

WALKING INSTRUCTIONS - Exit the underground station following signs for Tower of London. Descend steps to pass one of the last remaining sections of the Roman wall around the city, before passing through a tunnel to the Tower of London. If you are visiting this, turn right to the shop and ticket office. After you visit, turn left along the Thames Path towards Tower Bridge, and ascend steps. If going straight to Tower Bridge, turn left and soon ascend steps to the road and turn right to walk across the bridge.

The Tower of London.

TOWER OF LONDON - ***London's and England's most visited building. Here for over 900 years much of the history of England has been witnessed. Founded by William the Conqueror it houses the Crown Jewels, famed for the Yeoman Warders (Beefeaters), where Anne Boleyn was executed, where Guy Fawkes was interrogated, and where many traitors were imprisoned over the centuries in the Bloody Tower. For 700 years and still continuing is the Ceremony of Keys. Limited tickets are available for this daily custom - you write in advance to the Governor of the Tower. The Chief Yoeman Warder in a scarlet Tudor Coat, carries a lantern and accompanied by a foot guard escort arrive at the gates at preciously 9.53 p.m.***

TOWER BRIDGE - *Built in the late 19th. century (1894), this masterpiece of Victorian craftsmanship and ingenuity, is one of London's most famous landmarks. Although the docks are no longer closeby, the bridge still opens about 900 times a year to let big ships through; they have to give 24 hours notice. The bridge takes three minutes to lift open. You have stunning views as you walk across. Tower Bridge Exhibition - open daily.*

Walking across Tower Bridge.

The view of the Thames from Tower Bridge to the "Egg" and HMS Belfast.

Cross the bridge passing the Tower Bridge Exhibition entrance and at its immediate end turn right and descend steps to the Thames Path. Keep straight along Queens Walk and pass the oval shaped - "the egg" - City Hall (Greater London Authority Headquarters). Continue on beside the Thames with views back to Tower Bridge and Tower of London across the water, to HMS Belfast.

HMS BELFAST - ***Launched in 1938, it is the last surviving example of 20th. century big gunned warship - Cruiser. Saw considerable action during World War II and the Korean War. In 1971 it was saved for the nation and has nine decks to explore. The guns had a 14 mile range; the ship could travel at a top speed of 32 knots and 800 men manned her.***

Almost level with the prow, turn left along Battle Bridge Lane or alternatively walk through the Hays Galleria, with shops and restaurants, to Tooley Street. To the left is the Shipwright Arms and in front, Winston Churchill's Battle of Britain Exhibition. Turn right and soon pass the London Dungeon exhibition.

WINSTON CHURCHILL'S BATTLE OF BRITAIN - ***A glimpse of what it was like during the last war.***

LONDON DUNGEON - ***Like a chamber of horrors, you can see hangings, murders, Queen's being beheaded, and notorious people being taken through Traitor's Gate into the Tower of London.***

Continue along Tooley Street -

GREAT FIRE OF TOOLEY STREET, 1861 - ***In the 19th. century there were many large warehouses here full of material. The fire that swept through them lasted two weeks and was the biggest fire in London since the Great Fire 1666; and killed more people. One of them was the Superintendent of the London Fire Engine Establishment, James Braidwood, who died when a warehouse blew up. His death was a contributing factor in the creation of the London Fire Brigade in 1866.***

A little further along Tooley Street you pass Hays Wharf, and another historical plaque.

HAYS WHARF - ***Created by Alexander Hay in 1651, the present building of 1856 was built by Sir William Cubbitt. The large warehouse stored almost everything, except tobacco, specialising in tea. Cold Storage was pioneered here and was known as "London's Larder", for 75% of London's needs of bacon, butter, cheese and canned meat were kept here.***

Southwark Cathedral.

Continue on along Tooley Street past the London Bridge Hospital to London Bridge - Borough High Street (A13) and The Barrowboy and banker Inn opposite. Cross and turn left and descend steps to Green Dragon Court (restaurant/cafe), and keep Southwark Cathedral on your immediate right. Follow the edge of the grounds round to your right and cathedral entrance.

SOUTHWARK CATHEDRAL - ***The present building dates from the 13th. century, being an Augustinian Priory. It wasn't until 1905 that it became a Cathedral. Among the many memorials is one to William Shakespeare and John Gower - the first English Poet - who died in 1408. Another is to Lionel Lockyer, a famous quack doctor known for pills. Near the south-west door is a more recent memorial to the 51 people who lost their young lives in the Marchioness tragedy, on the Thames, in 1989.***

Continue round from the cathedral, soon bearing left to Pickford's Wharf, the Golden Hinde and the Old Thameside Inn.

THE GOLDEN HINDE - ***Moored in the St. Mary Overie Dock. The boat is a full size replica of Sir Francis Drake's 16th. century Tudor galleon. Like its original it has sailed round the world and done some 140,000 miles. The boat has five decks and a 14 cannon gun deck. On the original boat, Sir Francis Drake circled the world - 1577 - 1580 - and in 1581, Queen Elizabeth the First, knighted Drake on board. The Queen ordered the ship be preserved and became the world's first maritime museum.***

Notice by dock, from the 16th. century -

"This dock is a free landing place at which the parishioners of St. Saviours Parish are entitled to land goods free of toll."

Just beyond the Golden Hinde towards the River Thames is a stone plaque detailing the story of St. Mary Overie and the founding of a convent; the birth of Southwall Cathedral.

Continue left then right along Clink Street to pass on the left, the remains of Winchester Palace.

WINCHESTER PALACE - ***Although only a few ruins now, notably part of the Great Hall and Rose window, it was once a large palace founded by the Bishop's of Winchester in the 12th. century. They had great influence on this side of the Thames and the complex was the largest and most important in medieval London.***

The Golden Hinde.

Continue a little further along Clink Street to Clink Prison, on the left.

CLINK PRISON - ***Owned by the Bishops of Winchester, who also ran the red light district here! Between 1151 - 1780, it was a notorious medieval prison and where the name "clink" in jail come from. Here debtors, prostitutes and both Catholic and Protestants martyrs were held in very primitive conditions.***

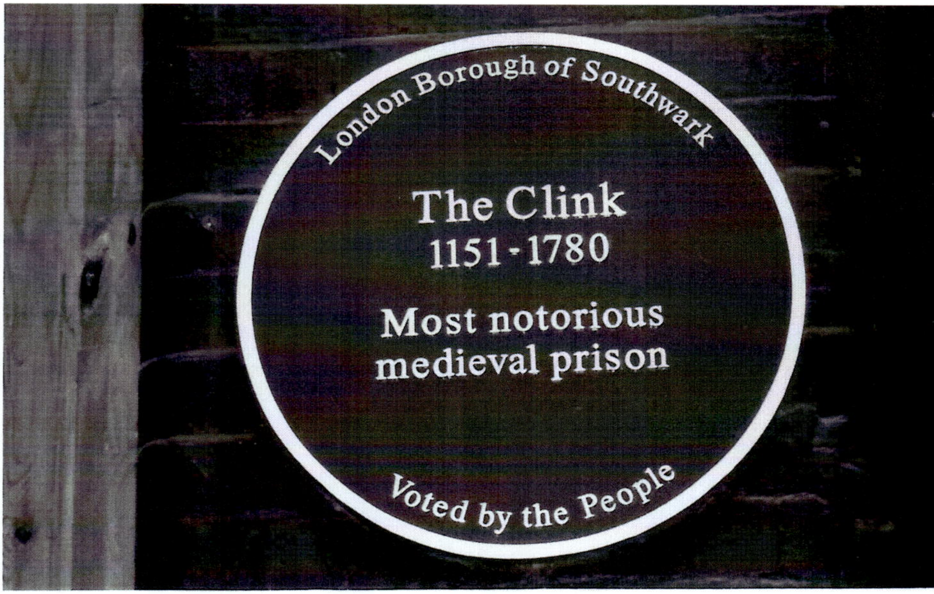

A few yards later reach the Vinopollis - City of Wine.

VINOPOLLIS CITY OF WINE - ***You can have a drink and meal here or take the wine tour.***

Turn right and left past The Anchor Inn and pass under Southwark Bridge, past numerous cafe's and restaurant's on your left, along Bankside to Shakespeare's Globe Theatre and Museum on the left.

WILLIAM SHAKESPEARE - ***The present Globe Theatre is close to the site of the orginal where Shakespeare worked until 1611 and is perfect replica of the originl buildingand opened in 1999. Shaespeare - England and the World's most famous playwright. Who cannot of heard of - Romeo and Juillet or The Taming of the Shrew? His plays are acted here - perhaps get a ticket?***

Continue a little further and on your left is 49, St. Cardinal's Wharf.

49, CARDINAL'S WHARF - ***Sir Christopher Wren stayed here while building St. Paul's and Catherine of Aragon when she first landed in London, stayed overnight here. She later became Henry 8th. wife first wife.***

The Globe Theatre.

A few yards more before turning left to cross the Millennium Bridge; just ahead is the Tate Modern Gallery.

TATE MODERN GALLERY - ***Formerly the Bankside Power Station, but converted to a magnificent 20th. century gallery. Deservedly it is one of London's most visited places.***

The Millenium Bridge and the Tate Modern Gallery.

MILLENNIUM BRIDGE - ***Designed by Norman Foster and Anthony Caro, the low slung bridge is an instant hit and as you walk across you have impressive views of the river and ahead to St. Paul's Cathedral.***

At the end of the bridge descend the steps on the left (Peter's Hill) to the River Thames and turn right along Paul's Walk, part of the northern Thames Path. At Blackfriars Bridge ascend steps, as signed for the Blackfriars Underground Station and keep ahead to the station.

WIGS & PENS - 3 MILES

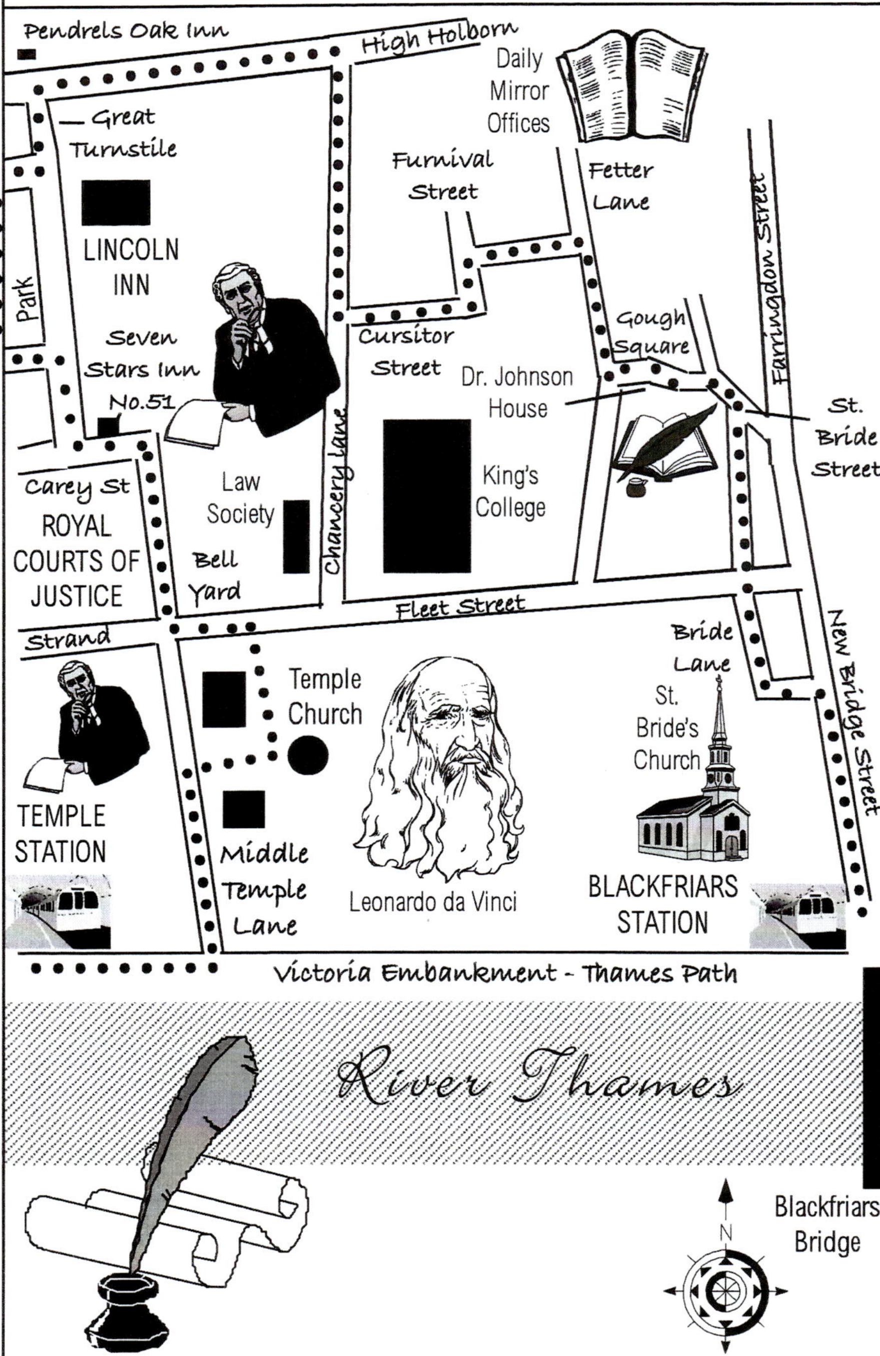

WIGS AND PENS
- 3 miles
- allow 2 to 3 hours

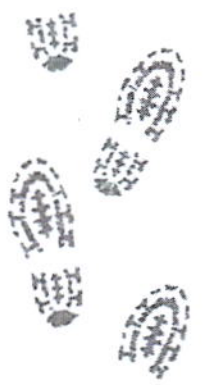

***Basic route** - Temple Underground Station - Victoria Embankment - Middle Temple Lane - Temple Church - Fleet Street - Royal Courts of Justice - Bell Yard - Royal College of Surgeons - Lincoln Inn Fields Park - Sir John Soane's Museum - High Holborn - London Silver Vaults - Fetter Lane - Dr. Johnson's House - St. Bridge Street - St. Bride's Church, New Bridge Street - Blackfriars Underground Station.*

***Start** - Temple Station Underground Station - Circle & District Line.*
***End** - Blackfriars Station Underground Station - Circle & District Line.*

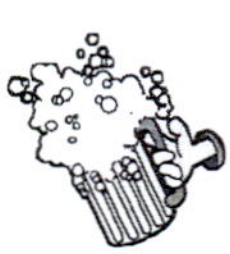

***Inns** - in walking order - The Old Bank of England, Fleet Street. Seven Stars, Carey Lane. The Ships Tavern, Gate Street; just off the route. Pendrels Oak Inn, High Holborn. Blue Anchor Inn, Norwich Street. The Cartoonist, Little New Street. The Punch Tavern, New Bridge Street.*

***Coffee/Cafe** - Numerous along the route.*

***Best time to do it** - Weekdays.*

ABOUT THE WALK - As the title suggests you pass many solicitors and barrister's chambers during the first half this walk. The second half ventures into the writers and press world, as you pass Dr. Johnson's House, Associated Press offices and St. Bride's church, the Printer's church of Fleet Street. Near the start you pass the Templar church featured in "The Da Vinci Code", book and film.

WALKING INSTRUCTIONS - Exit Temple Station to the Victoria Embankment. Keep to the lefthand side of the road past Temple Gardens and Temple Place to Middle Temple Lane. As path signed for the Temple Church turn left and enter one of the four "inns", the chambers of numerous barristers.

Pass Crown Office Row and soon after turn right (King's Bench Walk), as signed, for the Temple Church.

TEMPLE CHURCH - ***Built by the Knights Templar between 1161 - 1185, is said to be similar to the Holy Sepulchre church in Jerusalem. The circular church is the only one left in London. Inside are numerous effigy's of 12th. century knights. Around the walls are grotesque head carvings. In the middle of the paved area, outside is a single column with a templar knight on top; where is stands is the place where the Great Fire of London, in 1666 stopped. The ornate western doorway is Norman.***

Turn left in front of the entrance door and soon pass the western door on your right, and continue ahead to Fleet Street. Turn and then right along Bell Yard, but before doing so walk along Fleet Street/The Strand to pass the entrance to the Royal Courts of Justice and a little further on your left by a cafe is Twining's shop; a little further is the RAF church - St. Clements Danes - and monument to Dr. Samuel Johnson.

Dr. Samuel Johnson Monument, outside St. Clement's church (RAF).

TWINING'S - *Thomas Twining (1675 - 1741) founded the House of Twining here in 1706, when he bought Toms Coffee House. Here, he introduced tea and the following year was selling tea from his shop, called the Golden Lion. His grandson, Richard Twining (1749-1824) built the impressive doorway in 1787. Above can be seen the Golden Lion and two Chinese figures. These are made from a secret recipe and despite being over 200 years old, have withstood rain, frost and the blitz. Twining can safely be said the oldest company still in existence, to have traded continuously on the same site and by the same family - some 300 years.*

ROYAL COURTS OF JUSTICE - ***Designed by G. E. Street in 1874, the Great Hall has an exhibition of legal attire and a list of cases being heard that day.***

Retrace your steps back to Bell Yard and turn left along it past more chambers to Carey Street. Turn left and pass the Seven Stars Inn and immediately after is No. 51 - The Wig Box. Turn right just after along Serie Street to Lincoln Fields Inn and park. On the right is Lincoln's Inn, another famous barrister location, with a chapel.

The Royal Courts of Justice.

No. 51 - The Wig Box.

LINCOLN INN - ***Over the wall can be seen the Court building, which dates from the 15th. century***

Cross to the entrance to Lincoln Fields Park and walk left around it. To your left is the Royal College of Surgeons Museum. Pass tennis courts on your right and just after on your left is a bust to John Hunter - 1728-1793 - the founder of scientific surgery, with more details in the museum opposite. At the next corner of the park - north-western point - you can either continue right in the park or exit to the road and turn right along it. Straight ahead at the end of Gate Street is the Ship Tavern. Turn right along Lincoln Fields Inn and pass Sir John Soane's Museum and No. 20-23, the former Royal Canadian Air Force HQ - December 1941 - July 1946. Just after turn left along Great Turnstile to High Holborn road, opposite Pendrels Oak Inn.

SIR JOHN SOANE'S MUSEUM - ***Sir John Soane - 1753-1837 - designed the Bank of England. He was an avid collector of art and admission is free - Tuesday to Saturday - 10 a.m. to 5 p.m. This is one of the secret gems of London and well worth a visit to see the house and contents.***

Turn right along HIgh Holborn and right again along Chancery Lane. Pass the London Silver Vaults and it is worth turning left along Southampton Buildings to see the former Patent Office building. Continue along Chancery Lane to Cursitor Street and turn left. Opposite is a blue plaque to John Thurloe. Further down Chancery lane is the Law Society Offices and the imposing Kings College and Maugham Library.

JOHN THURLOE (Cromwell Association) - 1616-1668.
Secretary of State 1652
Bencher of Lincoln Fields Inn 1654
Lived in old square at various times until his death.

Walk along Curister Street past Quality Court and Printers Ink Court and turn left along Furnival Street for a few yards before turning right by the Castle Inn, along Norwich Street.

THE CASTLE INN, NORWICH STREET - ***In the 14th. century the inn was part of the original Lincoln Inn, and there has been an inn on this site for 700 years.***

At the end of Norwich Street pass the Associated Press office and reach Fetter Lane. Turn right - to your left are the Daily Mirror Offices. Pass the Blue Anchor Inn, and Rolls Building and monument to John Wilkes on the left.

JOHN WILKES - 1727-1797
- M.P. and Lord Mayor.
"A champion of English Freedom."

Just after turn left into Pemberton Row - signed for Dr. Johnson House - and follow it left and then right to Gough Square and Dr. Johnson's house.

DR. SAMUEL JOHNSON - 1709-1784. ***Lived here at No. 17. Well know writer and famously toured the Hebrides with Boswell. He wrote the first comprehensive English Dictionary. Museum open weekdays - 11 a.m. to 5 p.m.***

Turn left through the square and then right along Little New Street and pass the Cartoonist Inn. Cross Shoe Lane to the right along St. Bridge Street and right along Poppins Court to Fleet Street. Cross to your left to Bride lane - to your left is the Punch Tavern; a reminder of Punch Magazine. Reach St. Bride's Church - access is along the path on the right.

ST. BRIDE'S CHURCH - ***The church has been associated with printing for over 500 years; in 1500 AD Wynkyn de Worde set up a printing press in the churchyard. Named after the 5th. century Irish saint, St. Bride. Records show that during one week in 1665, when the plague was ravishing, 238 parishioners died from it. The church was destroyed a year later in the Great Fire. Sir Christopher Wren designed the present building with the tallest spire - 234 feet, completed in 1703. The tiered spire was the inspiration for a nearby baker in the 18th. century who***

produced the first tired wedding cake. It is only in recent times that the Crypt was uncovered showing the church foundations dating back to Roman and Saxon times. It is well worth visiting this to see more of London's early story.

Follow the lane left to New Bridge Street and cross over and turn right to Blackfriars Underground Station; just before the Blackfriars Inn.

Dr. Samuel Johnson House, Gough Square.

THE HOT SPOTS - 2 1/2 MILES

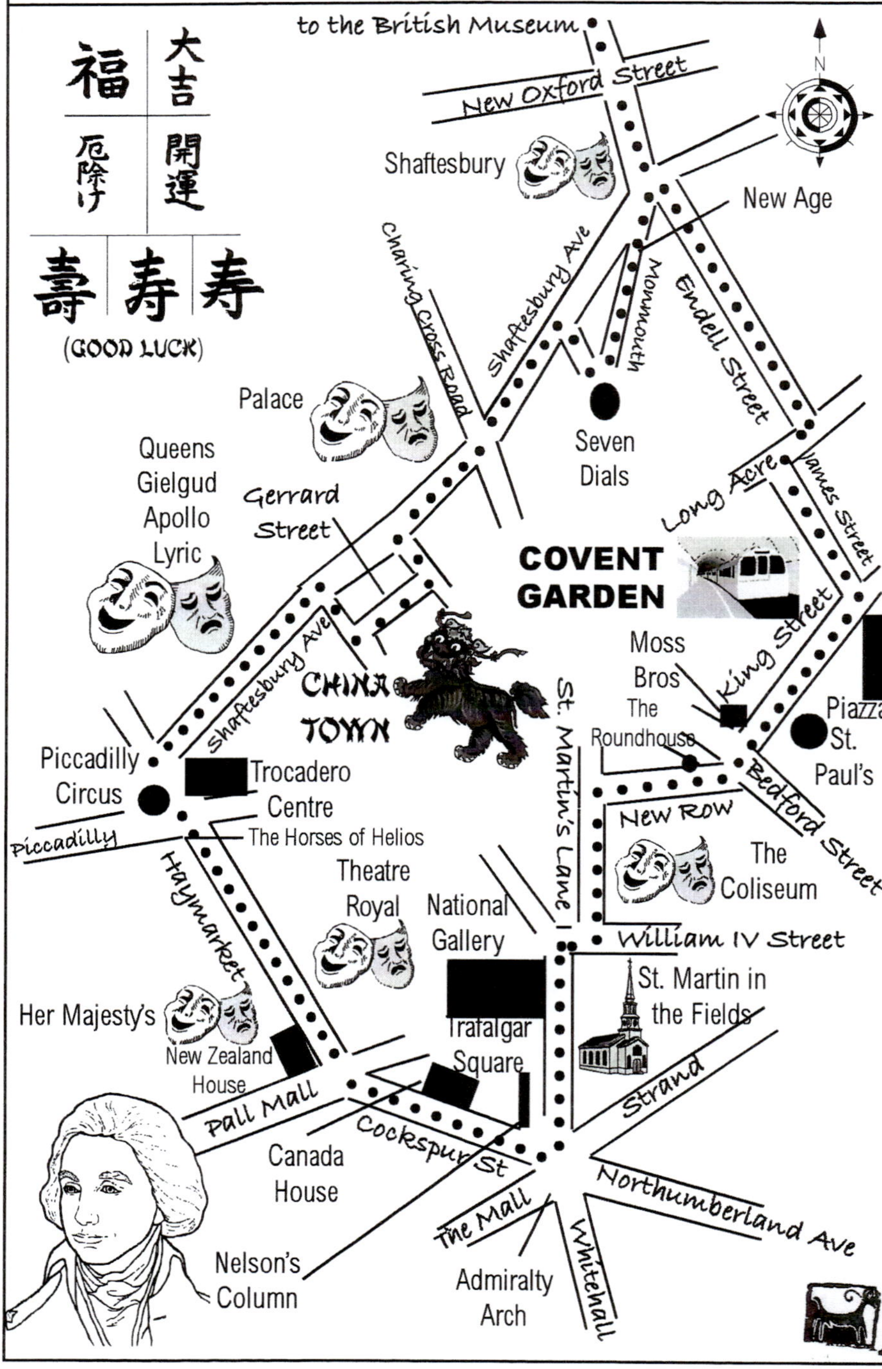

THE HOT SPOTS
- 2 1/2 MILES
- Allow 2 to 3 hours.

Basic route - Covent Garden Underground Station - Covent Garden Piazza - St. Paul's Church - New Row - St. Martin's Lane - St. Martin in the Fields Church - Trafalgar Square - Cockspur Street - Haymarket - Piccadilly Circus - Shaftesbury Avenue - China Town - - Seven Dials - Cambridge Circus - St. Giles - Long Acre - Covent Garden.

Optional - 5 mins extension from St. Giles to the British Museum.

Start and end - Covent Garden Underground Station (Piccadilly Line).

Inns - Numerous on the walk, including in walking order - No.1 Roundhouse, New Road. The Angel & Crown, and The Chandos Inn, St. Martin's Lane. The St. James Tavern, Shaftesbury Avenue. The Crown, Seven Dials. The Cross Keys Inn, Endell Street.

Cafe/Coffee - Numerous throughout the route.

Restaurants - Covent Garden, Piccadilly Circus and China Town.

ABOUT THE WALK - After the six preceding walks here is a leisurely one to some of the key London sights - Covent Garden, Trafalgar Square and Nelson's Column, Piccadilly Circus and London's China Town. But that is only part of walk, for you pass fascinating churches and much of Theatre land. You can shop for souvenirs, visit a few lesser known places and London's premier New Age Shop with resident Psychic's. If galleries and museums are your forte, you pass the National Portrait Gallery and National Gallery and just off the route is the British Museum. Like all the walks there is much to pick and choose as you walks the streets of London....enjoy!

WALKING INSTRUCTIONS - Gaining the street from the underground turn right, along James Street to the Covent Garden Piazza. To your left is the Royal Opera House, where you can take a "behind the scenes" tour. James Street before the Piazza is a popular area for Street artists, as in front of St. Paul's church, to your right and on your route. While inside the Piazza, apart from shops and cafe's you can listen to music and opera.

Covent Garden Street Artist/Statue.

COVENT GARDEN MARKET - ***Voted London's premier shopping experience, with over forty shops and specialist stalls. Designed by Indigo Jones for the Earl of Bedford.***

Turn right towards St. Paul's Church and on its lefthand side can be seen an inscription recording -

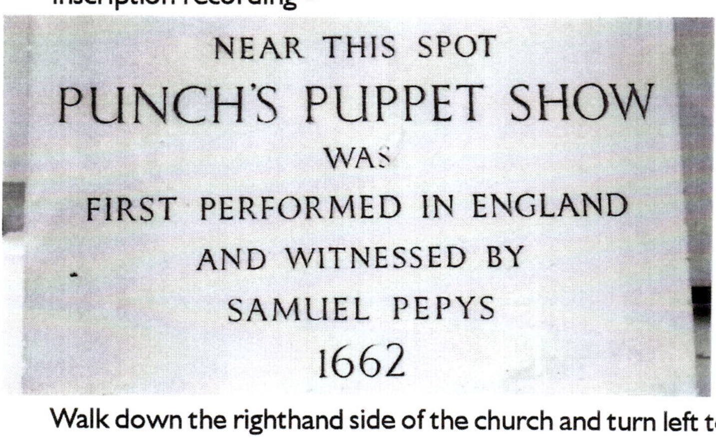

Opposite on the western side of the Piazza is the aptly named Punch and Judy balcony bar.

Walk down the righthand side of the church and turn left to enter the church.

ST. PAUL'S CHURCH - ***Designed by Indigo Jones, who was the Surveyor of Works to Charles 1st. It is said that the Earl wanted a simple church like a barn, so this must be the most impressive barn ever made! Work started in 1631 and was completed in 1633. Known as the Actor's church and a walk around inside will bring you to many famous actor's and actress's memorials, including, Vivienne Leigh, Richard Watts, Laurence Harvey, Hattie Jacques, Sir Noel Coward, Kenneth More and Gracie Fields.***

Turn right out of the door and keep straight ahead through a passage to King Street and turn left along it. In a short distance on the right is a blue plaque to-

"Thomas Arne 1710 - 1778.
Composer, lived here."

A little further on the right is the famous Moss Bros, formal clothing shop.

Moss Bros.

Cross Garrick Street into New Row and keep straight ahead and pass No.1 Roundhouse.

ROUNDHOUSE - ***Opened in 1868 as the Petters Hotel and 75 years later became known as the Roundhouse - from its frontal shape, when bought by Wm. Younger in 1943.***

At the end of the Row on your left is the Anchor and Crown Inn. Turn left along St. Martin's Lane and enter theatre land; a theme that will continue for the remainder of the route. Pass the Duke of York Theatre and the impressive front of the Coliseum theatre.

THE LONDON COLISEUM - ***Opened in 1904 as a variety theatre. Sir Oswald Stoll the designer wanted a revolving dome on top but the authorities would not approve the scheme, and the circular top has flashing lights instead. Since 1968 the theatre has been the home of National Opera.***

Pass The Chandos Inn and at the end of the lane, cross to your right and left into St. Martins Place, passing the memorial to -

"Edith Cavell"
Brussels Dawn - Oct. 12th. 1915.
"Patriotism is not enough
I must have no hatred or bitterness for anyone."

Born 1865 and executed by the Germans in 1915. A nurse who helped many soldiers escape from Brussels in World War 1.

On you right is the National Portrait Gallery

NATIONAL GALLERY & PORTRAIT GALLERY - ***Open daily; free entrance. Founded in 1856 it houses more than 10,000 portraits, but only a fraction of them are on display at any one time. Further to the right is the National Gallery - open daily; free admission. With some 2,000 paintings by the world leading artists through the centuries, it is one of London's most popular galleries.***

Continue down St. Martin's Place and on your left is the fine church of St. Martin in the Fields.

Trafalgar Square and the National Gallery.

ST. MARTIN IN THE FIELDS - *When the first church was built here 700 years ago, it was as the name suggests, just fields and woodland, instead of looking over Trafalgar Square. The present church, the fourth here, was designed by James Gibbs (1682-1754) and was completed in 1726. A new design with corinthian columns and tower and steeple. Popular with Royalty and with their own Royal Box, George 1st., whose arms are in the outside front pediment, was the first churchwarden here and the only Monarch to have this position. The church is a popular concert venue.*

Walk around Trafalgar Square past Nelson's Monument and right along Cockspur Street. To your left is Admiralty Arch and the start of The Mall to Buckingham Palace.

ADMIRALTY ARCH - ***Built to honour Queen Victoria in 1910.***

TRAFALGAR SQUARE - ***Rallying centre for marches and speeches and for seeing in the New Year. There are monuments to George Washington and King George IV on horseback, but dominating everything is the 169ft. high, Nelson's Column; originally it was believed to be 185 ft. high. Built in 1843 with Admiral Nelson surveying his fleet; it commemorates his victory over Napoleon in 1805 off Cape Trafalgar in Spain. In 2006 it was cleaned and repaired at a cost of £420,000.***

George Washington Statue - Trafalgar Square. America's first President.

Walk along Cockspur Street with Canada House on your right, built in 1827 and designed by Robert Smirke. Reaching Pall Mall cross to your right to walk along Haymarket. On your left is the High Commission of New Zealand - New Zealand House - with a blue plaque on its side -

A little further on your left is Her Majesty's Theatre - ***"Founded in 1897 by Herbert tree, Actor and directed by him until his death in 1917."*** On the right is the Theatre Royal and a little further on the left Cineworld. Approaching Piccadilly Circus on your right is the Criterion Theatre and the amusement area - Trocadero Centre. On the lefthand corner is the statue and waterfall of, ***"The Horses of Helios".***

Theatre Royal, Haymarket.

Piccadilly Circus - Eros Fountain.

Turn left along the southern side of Piccadilly Circus, with its large neon signs to the Eros Fountain.

EROS FOUNTAIN - ***This not its real name for when it was placed here in 1893 it was the Angel of Christian Charity and dedicated to Lord Shaftesbury a philanthropist and social reformer. Later the statue was thought to be eros, the God of Love, and the name has stuck ever since. The name Piccadilly comes from the 17th. century fashion her of wearing stiff collars known as "Picadils". The local tailor here, at the time, had a brisk trade, until they went out of fashion.***

Bear half right to walk along Shaftesbury Avenue, passing the St. James Tavern on your left and just after up a side street the famous Windmill Theatre and Soho beyond. Pass the Lyric Theatre, Apollo Theatre, Gielgud Theatre and Queens Theatre before turning right along Wardour Street. Turn left into Gerrard Street and enter China Town; notice the road signs are in English and Chinese. The best time to come here is during Chinese New Year. Walk past shops and many restaurant's to the other entrance gate and turn left back to Shaftesbury Avenue.

Gerrard Place and entrance gate to Gerrard Street, the main street of China Town.

Turn right and pass the Palace Theatre to Cambridge Circus. Keep straight ahead now along a smaller Shaftesbury Avenue to the Odeon Cinema and turn right along Mercer Street.

No. 166A Shaftesbury Avenue - Chinese church in London. The building was the former Soho Baptist church built in 1887.

Reach The Crown Inn on the left and the monument of Seven Dials.

SEVEN DIALS - ***Built in 1694 by Edward Pierce and Thomas Neale. Removed from Seven Dials and rebuilt here in 1773.***

Turn left along Monmouth Street and pass on the right, London's Physic Shop and New Age Centre. Rejoin Shaftesbury Avenue and to your right is an Astrology Centre. A few yards later and opposite Shaftesbury Theatre, turn right along Endell Street.

To your left, as signed, is a five minute walk to the British Museum. If you have time it is extremely well worth while to visit - free - and see the exhibits and spectacular library and covered piazza.

The Cross Keys Inn, Endell Street.

Pass The Cross Keys Inn and at the end of Endell Street near the junction with Long Acre, on the building on the right can be see a ***Queen's bust set in the wall. This is a reminder that the site was once the Queens Theatre between 1867 - 1878. Although only running for eleven years it was a popular venue.***

Turn right along Long Acre and in a few yards left into James Street and back at the Covent Garden Underground Station.

Alas, like the book, the walk ends here.........but more walks are on the way!

WALK RECORD PAGE

Date walked -

The Royal Palaces - 6 1/2 miles ....

The Good and the Gracious - 3 miles ....

Monks, Murder, Punishment & Poetry - 1 1/2 mile.s.......................................

The Great Fire of London, 1666 - 5 miles ....

Bridges, Boats & Dungeons - 3 miles ....

Wigs & Pens - 3 miles ....

The Hot Spots - 2 1/2 miles ....

Some Important annual dates -

London has a packed programme of events, customs and pagentry throughout the year and the following pages are just a sprinkling of some of them.

February - CHINESE NEW YEAR IN CHINA TOWN.

April - *The London Marathon.*

June - *The Queen's Birthday Gun Salute in Hyde Park.*

- *A Walk for Life - Aids/Hiv 6 mile Chairty walk in central London, organised by Crusaid.*

August - **THE NOTTING HILL CARNIVAL.**

September - *The Thames Festival - South Bank.*

November - *The Lord Mayor's Show - Mansion House & St. Paul's.*

THE CHINESE NEW YEAR.

The London Marathon.

The Queen's Birthday Salute.

Walk for Life - and author with his medal!

The Lord Mayor's Show.

The Lord Mayor's Coach and Pikemen.

One of the many floats - "The Legal Eagles"!

OTHER NORTH LONDON WALK BOOKS
by JOHN N. MERRILL

SHORT CIRCULAR WALKS ON THE RIVER LEE NAVIGATION - Northern Volume - Ponder's End - Hertford. 64 pages, 23 photographs, 10 detailed maps and walks. History notes.
- ISBN 1-903627-68-0 @ £7.95

WALKING THE RIVER LEE NAVIGATION - VOL 1 & 2.

SHORT CIRCULAR WALKS ON THE NEW RIVER & SOUTH EAST HERTFORDSHIRE
11 walks - 5 to 10 miles long between Waltham Cross and Hertford; many on the New River. New revised and enlarged edition 68 pages, 24 photographs , 13 detailed maps. History notes.
ISBN 1-903627-69-9 @ £7.95

SHORT CIRCULAR WALKS IN EPPING FOREST
10 circular walks 6 to 18 miles long. Combined they explore the whole forest and its surrounding area. 68 pages. 12 maps. 30 photographs. History notes.
ISBN 1-903627-72-9 @ £7.95

LONG CIRCULAR WALKS IN EASTERN HERTFORDSHIRE
9 walks - 15 to 20 miles long. Beautiful unspoilt walking in rolling countryside full of historical interest. £9.95
ISBN 978-0-9553691-7-9

LONG CIRCULAR WALKS IN WESTERN HERTFORDSHIRE
- 9 long walks - 15 to 20 miles.. 112 pages. Wire bound. 55 photographs. 20detailed maps. £9.95 ISBN 978-0-955651113

SHORT CIRCULAR WALKS AROUND HERTFORD.
3 historical Town walks and four country walks.
ISBN 978-0-955651I-7-5 £9.95

SHORT CIRCULAR WALKS ON THE RIVER STORT NAVIGATION
8 circular walks; 1 End to End walk. Full history and photographic study of this peaceful waterway. 92 pages. 68 photographhgs. 12 maps. ISBN 1-903627- 73-7 £9.95

SHORT CIRCULAR WALKS ON THE RIVER LEE NAVIGATION - Southern Volume -
Limehouse basin to Hackney Marsh. 5 walks on the Regent Canal, Hertford Union and Limehouse Cut. Including Three Mills and its rivers. The guide also details a 28 mile End to End walk along the Navigation. 68 pages. 10 maps, 30 photographs.
ISBn 1-903627-74-5 £7.95

EPPING FOREST CHALLENGE WALK - 21 MILES.
Starts and ends at Waltham Abbey and takes in the whole forest. 44 pages. 6 maps. 10 photos £5.95
ISBN 978-0-9553691-0-0

"St. ALBANS WAY" - 26 mile Pilgrims walk from Waltham Abbey to St. Alban's Cathedral.
£5.95
ISBN 978-0-9553691-3-1

NORTH LONDON - THE THREE BOROUGH CHALLENGE WALK - 21 MILES
A walk linking together the three boroughs of Enfield, Barnet and Haringey.
A magnificent countryside walk. Certificate for the successful.
A5. 40 pages. Full colour book.
ISBN 978-0-955651I-9-9
£5.95

NEW - SHORT CIRCULAR WALKS AROUND BISHOP'S STORTFORD

OTHER BOOKS by Revd. John N. Merrill

CIRCULAR WALK GUIDES -

SHORT CIRCULAR WALKS IN THE PEAK DISTRICT - Vols. 1 to 9
CIRCULAR WALKS IN WESTERN PEAKLAND
SHORT CIRCULAR WALKS IN THE STAFFORDSHIRE MOORLANDS
SHORT CIRCULAR WALKS - TOWNS & VILLAGES OF THE PEAK DISTRICT
SHORT CIRCULAR WALKS AROUND MATLOCK
SHORT CIRCULAR WALKS IN "PEAK PRACTICE COUNTRY."
SHORT CIRCULAR WALKS IN THE DUKERIES
SHORT CIRCULAR WALKS IN SOUTH YORKSHIRE
SHORT CIRCULAR WALKS IN SOUTH DERBYSHIRE
SHORT CIRCULAR WALKS AROUND BUXTON
SHORT CIRCULAR WALKS AROUND WIRKSWORTH
SHORT CIRCULAR WALKS IN THE HOPE VALLEY
40 SHORT CIRCULAR WALKS IN THE PEAK DISTRICT
CIRCULAR WALKS ON KINDER & BLEAKLOW
SHORT CIRCULAR WALKS IN SOUTH NOTTINGHAMSHIRE
SHORT CIRCULAR WALKS IN CHESHIRE
SHORT CIRCULAR WALKS IN WEST YORKSHIRE
WHITE PEAK DISTRICT AIRCRAFT WRECKS
CIRCULAR WALKS IN THE DERBYSHIRE DALES
SHORT CIRCULAR WALKS FROM BAKEWELL
SHORT CIRCULAR WALKS IN LATHKILL DALE
CIRCULAR WALKS IN THE WHITE PEAK
SHORT CIRCULAR WALKS IN EAST DEVON
SHORT CIRCULAR WALKS AROUND HARROGATE
SHORT CIRCULAR WALKS IN CHARNWOOD FOREST
SHORT CIRCULAR WALKS AROUND CHESTERFIELD
SHORT CIRCULAR WALKS IN THE YORKS DALES - Vol 1 - Southern area.
SHORT CIRCULAR WALKS IN THE AMBER VALLEY (Derbyshire)
SHORT CIRCULAR WALKS IN THE LAKE DISTRICT
SHORT CIRCULAR WALKS IN THE NORTH YORKSHIRE MOORS
SHORT CIRCULAR WALKS IN EAST STAFFORDSHIRE
LONG CIRCULAR WALKS IN THE PEAK DISTRICT - Vol.1 to 5.
DARK PEAK AIRCRAFT WRECK WALKS
LONG CIRCULAR WALKS IN THE STAFFORDSHIRE MOORLANDS
LONG CIRCULAR WALKS IN CHESHIRE
WALKING THE TISSINGTON TRAIL
WALKING THE HIGH PEAK TRAIL
WALKING THE MONSAL TRAIL & SETT VALLEY TRAILS
PEAK DISTRICT WALKING - TEN "TEN MILER'S" - Vol 1 and 2.
CLIMB THE PEAKS OF THE PEAK DISTRICT
PEAK DISTRICT WALK A MONTH Vols One,Two, Three, Four, Five & Six
TRAIN TO WALK Vol. One - The Hope Valley Line
DERBYSHIRE LOST VILLAGE WALKS -Vol One and Two.
CIRCULAR WALKS IN DOVEDALE AND THE MANIFOLD VALLEY
CIRCULAR WALKS AROUND GLOSSOP
WALKING THE LONGDENDALE TRAIL
WALKING THE UPPER DON TRAIL
SHORT CIRCULAR WALKS IN CANNOCK CHASE
CIRCULAR WALKS IN THE DERWENT VALLEY
WALKING THE TRAILS OF NORTH-EAST DERBYSHIRE
WALKING THE PENNINE BRIDLEWAY & CIRCULAR WALKS
SHORT CIRCULAR WALKS ON THE NEW RIVER & SOUTH-EAST HERTFORDSHIRE
SHORT CIRCULAR WALKS IN EPPING FOREST
SHORT CIRCULAR WALKS AROUND SAFFRON WALDEN
WALKING THE STREETS OF LONDON
LONG CIRCULAR WALKS IN EASTERN HERTFORDSHIRE
LONG CIRCULAR WALKS IN WESTERN HERTFORDSHIRE
WALKS IN THE LONDON BOROUGH OF ENFIELD
WALKS IN THE LONDON BOROUGH OF BARNET
WALKS IN THE LONDON BOROUGH OF HARINGEY
WALK IN THE LONDON BOROUGH OF WALTHAM FOREST
SHORT CIRCULAR WALKS AROUND HERTFORD
THE BIG WALKS OF LONDON
SHORT CIRCULAR WALKS AROUND BISHOP'S STORTFORD
SHORT CIRCULAR WALKS AROUND EPPING DISTRICT
CIRCULAR WALKS IN THE BOROUGH OF BROXBOURNE
LONDON INTERFAITH WALKS - Vol 1 and Vol. 2
LONG CIRCULAR WALKS IN THE NORTH CHILTERNS
SHORT CIRCULAR WALKS IN EASTERN HERTFORDSHIRE
WORCESTERSHIRE VILLAGE WALKS by Des Wright
WARWICKSHIRE VILLAGE WALKS by Des Wright
WALKING AROUND THE ROYAL PARKS OF LONDON
WALKS IN THE LONDON BOROUGH OF CHELSEA AND ROYAL KENSINGTON

CANAL WALKS -

VOL 1 - DERBYSHIRE & NOTTINGHAMSHIRE
VOL 2 - CHESHIRE & STAFFORDSHIRE
VOL 3 - STAFFORDSHIRE
VOL 4 - THE CHESHIRE RING
VOL 5 - THE GRANTHAM CANAL
VOL 6 - SOUTH YORKSHIRE
VOL 7 - THE TRENT & MERSEY CANAL
VOL 8 - WALKING THE DERBY CANAL RING
VOL 9 - WALKING THE LLANGOLLEN CANAL
VOL 10 - CIRCULAR WALKS ON THE CHESTERFIELD CANAL
VOL 11 - CIRCULAR WALKS ON THE CROMFORD CANAL
Vol.13 - SHORT CIRCULAR WALKS ON THE RIVER LEE NAVIGATION -Vol. 1 - North
Vol. 14 - SHORT CIRCULAR WALKS ON THE RIVER STORT NAVIGATION
Vol.15 - SHORT CIRCULAR WALKS ON THE RIVER LEE NAVIGATION - Vol. 2 - South
Vol. 16 - WALKING THE CANALS OF LONDON
Vol 17 - WALKING THE RIVER LEE NAVIGATION
Vol. 20 - SHORT CIRCULAR WALKS IN THE COLNE VALLEY
Vol 21 - THE BLACKWATER & CHELMER NAVIGATION - End to End.
Vol. 22 - NOTTINGHAM'S LOST CANAL by Bernard Chell.
Vol. 23 - WALKING THE RIVER WEY & GODALMING NAVIAGTIONS END TO END
Vol.25 - WALKING THE GRAND UNION CANAL - LONDON TO BIRMINGHAM.

JOHN MERRILL DAY CHALLENGE WALKS

WHITE PEAK CHALLENGE WALK
THE HAPPY HIKER - WHITE PEAK - CHALLENGE WALK
DARK PEAK CHALLENGE WALK
PEAK DISTRICT END TO END WALKS
STAFFORDSHIRE MOORLANDS CHALLENGE WALK

JOHN MERRILL DAY CHALLENGE WALKS

WHITE PEAK CHALLENGE WALK
THE HAPPY HIKER - WHITE PEAK - CHALLENGE WALK No.2
DARK PEAK CHALLENGE WALK
PEAK DISTRICT END TO END WALKS
STAFFORDSHIRE MOORLANDS CHALLENGE WALK
THE LITTLE JOHN CHALLENGE WALK
YORKSHIRE DALES CHALLENGE WALK
NORTH YORKSHIRE MOORS CHALLENGE WALK
LAKELAND CHALLENGE WALK
THE RUTLAND WATER CHALLENGE WALK
MALVERN HILLS CHALLENGE WALK
THE SALTERiS WAY
THE SNOWDON CHALLENGE
CHARNWOOD FOREST CHALLENGE WALK
THREE COUNTIES CHALLENGE WALK (Peak District).
CAL-DER-WENT WALK
THE QUANTOCK WAY
BELVOIR WITCHES CHALLENGE WALK
THE CARNEDDAU CHALLENGE WALK
THE SWEET PEA CHALLENGE WALK
THE LINCOLNSHIRE WOLDS - BLACK DEATH - CHALLENGE WALK
JENNIFER'S CHALLENGE WALK
THE EPPING FOREST CHALLENGE WALK
THE THREE BOROUGH CHALLENGE WALK - NORTH LONDON
THE HERTFORD CHALLENGE WALK
THE BOSHAM CHALLENGE WALK
THE KING JOHN CHALLENGE WALK
THE NORFOLK BROADS CHALLENGE WALK
THE RIVER MIMRAM WALK
THE ISLE OF THANET CHHALENGE WALK
EAST DEVON CHALLENGE WALK

INSTRUCTION & RECORD -

HIKE TO BE FIT.....STROLLING WITH JOHN
THE JOHN MERRILL WALK RECORD BOOK
HIKE THE WORLD - John Merrill's guide to walking & Backpacking.

MULTIPLE DAY WALKS -

THE RIVERS'S WAY
PEAK DISTRICT: HIGH LEVEL ROUTE
PEAK DISTRICT MARATHONS
THE LIMEY WAY
THE PEAKLAND WAY
COMPO'S WAY by Alan Hiley
THE BRIGHTON WAY

COAST WALKS & NATIONAL TRAILS -

ISLE OF WIGHT COAST PATH
PEMBROKESHIRE COAST PATH
THE CLEVELAND WAY
WALKING ANGELSEY'S COASTLINE.
WALKING THE COASTLINE OF THE CHANNEL ISLANDS
THE ISLE OF MAN COASTAL PATH - "The Way of the Gull."
A WALK AROUND HAYLING ISLAND
A WALK AROUND THE ISLE OF SHEPPEY
A WALK AROUND THE ISLE OF JERSEY
WALKING AROUND THE ISLANDS OF ESSEX

DERBYSHIRE & PEAK DISTRICT HISTORICAL GUIDES -

A to Z GUIDE OF THE PEAK DISTRICT
DERBYSHIRE INNS - an A to Z guide
HALLS AND CASTLES OF THE PEAK DISTRICT & DERBYSHIRE
TOURING THE PEAK DISTRICT & DERBYSHIRE BY CAR
DERBYSHIRE FOLKLORE
PUNISHMENT IN DERBYSHIRE
CUSTOMS OF THE PEAK DISTRICT & DERBYSHIRE
WINSTER - a souvenir guide
ARKWRIGHT OF CROMFORD
LEGENDS OF DERBYSHIRE
DERBYSHIRE FACTS & RECORDS
TALES FROM THE MINES by Geoffrey Carr
PEAK DISTRICT PLACE NAMES by Martin Spray
DERBYSHIRE THROUGH THE AGES - Vol 1 -DERBYSHIRE IN PREHISTORIC TIMES
SIR JOSEPH PAXTON
FLORENCE NIGHTINGALE
JOHN SMEDLEY
BONNIE PRINCE CHARLIE & 20 mile walk.
THE STORY OF THE EARLS AND DUKES OF DEVONSHIRE

JOHN MERRILL'S MAJOR WALKS -

TURN RIGHT AT LAND'S END
WITH MUSTARD ON MY BACK
TURN RIGHT AT DEATH VALLEY
EMERALD COAST WALK
I CHOSE TO WALK - Why I walk etc.
A WALK IN OHIO - 1,310 miles around the Buckeye Trail.
I AM GUIDED - the story of John's wal;king life.

SKETCH BOOKS -

SKETCHES OF THE PEAK DISTRICT

COLOUR BOOK:-

THE PEAK DISTRICT.......something to remember her by.

OVERSEAS GUIDES -

HIKING IN NEW MEXICO - Vol I - The Sandia and Manzano Mountains.
Vol 2 - Hiking "Billy the Kid" Country.
Vol 4 - N.W. area - " Hiking Indian Country."
"WALKING IN DRACULA COUNTRY" - Romania.
WALKING THE TRAILS OF THE HONG KONG ISLANDS.

VISITOR GUIDES - MATLOCK . BAKEWELL. ASHBOURNE.

See all my books on -
www.johnmerrillwalkguides.co.uk

Pilgrim Guides -
www.thejohnmerrillministry.co.uk

LONDON PILGRIMAGE WALKS

In medieval times both royalty and layfolk undertook pilgrimages to several holy shrines - to St. Albans, Canterbury and Walsingham via Waltham Abbey. These three books trace the different routes and are walks not just exercise and health but for journeys of the soul and spirituality.

LONDON TO ST. ALBANS - 36 MILES

Starting from Westminster Abbey, the route takes you through North-West London, via more than 30 church's, chapels and places of worship. The basic route is via Regent's Park, Hampstead, Burnt Oak, Stanmore, Elstree and River Ver.

88 pages. 7 maps. 100 photographs. £9.95

ISBN 978-0-9560649-7-4

LONDON TO CANTERBURY - 75 MILES

Starting from Westminster Abbey the route is via Southark Cathedral and River Thames to Greenwich. Then Watling Street to Gravesend, Rochester, Sittingbourne and Faversham to Canterbury. Numerous churchs and historial features are passed.

140 pages. 15 maps. 120 photographs. £12.95

ISBN 978-0-9560649-6-7

LONDON TO WALSINGHAM - 174/194 MILES

Starting from Holborn or St. Magnus church, the route takes you up the Lee Valley to Waltham Abbey - a pilgrimage centre in its own right. Then onto Ware, Cottered, Royston, Newmarket, Mildenhall,Bury St. Edmunds, Brandon, Swaffham, Fakenham, the Slipper Chapel and Little Walsingham.

256 pages. 41 maps. 243 photographs. £14.95

ISBN 978-0-9564644-2-2

A WALK FOR PEACE - 10 MILES

A Buddhist themed walk from the Tibetan Peace Gardens beside the Imperial War Museum to Battersea Peace Pagoda and onto the Buddhapadipa temple. at Wimbledon.

20 pages. Colour photographs. £3.95

NEW LONDON WALK GUIDES

WALKING THE CANALS OF LONDON

Nine walks fully exploring - The Regents Canal, Grand Union Canal (Paddington Branch), River Thames and Isle of Dogs and the "London Canal Loop".
A5 wire bound. 108 pages. 13 maps. 95 b/w photographs.

£10.95 ISBN 978-0-9553691-2-4

WALKING THE STREETS OF LONDON

7 historical short walks - 2 to 6 miles long and allowing - 4 TO 5 HOURS - in the city with basic themes -

"The Great Fire', "Wigs & Pens".
The Good and Gracious".
"The Royal Palaces", "The Hot Spots",
"Bridges, Boats and Dungeons".
"Monks, murder, punishment and poetry".

A5 wire bound. 112 pages. 9 maps. 84 b/w photographs.

£10.95 ISBN 978-0-9553691-1-7

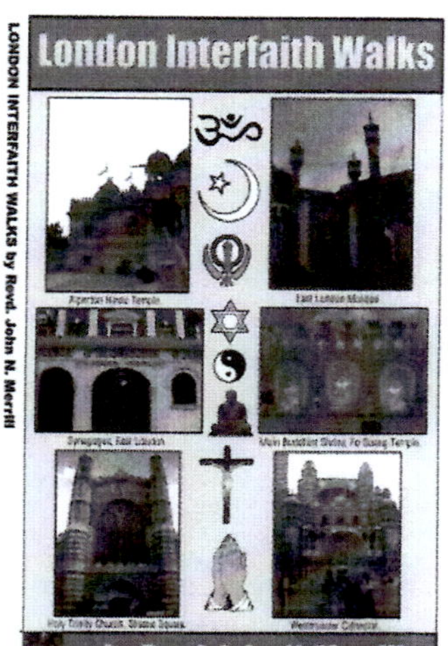

LONDON INTERFAITH WALKS

Seven walks in London to all the major religious sites.
Themed walks - Christian, Buddhist, Hindu etc.
. A5 Wire bound. 112 pages. 10 maps 130 photos.
£10.95
ISBN 978-0-9568044-3-3

See all our books on our website - www.johnmerrillwalkguides.com

Wherever you are, you are either
on or close to a
John Merrill Walk.
........enjoy!

WALKING THE PURE WAY

I believe a walk, whatever the distance, should be done on two feet, with basics of life on your back and map/gps in your hand. When I first started the thought of missing a section and using transport was the death knoll to the walk. I could not live with myself if I had missed a section.

Today when I walk to Santiago de Compestella on a 1,000 mile route, I am saddened that many walkers take a bus here and there, missing out a section that was "boring". I could never understand, at first, having overtook a walker, a few days later they were ahead of me. They had certainly not passed me. When I walked the Pacific Crest Trail in America. I walked it all despite deep snow in the Sierra's. Many who get there because of snow and closed trails, bus round, missing 300 miles or more of trail. I had snow and had to walk beneath the mountains for four days before finding a way in. It still meant that I had full-filled my plan and walked from Mexico to Canada un-aided. And having reached Canada flew back to the High Sierra's and climbed them all. Then I went home feeling complete.'

Similarly on the Appalachian Trail, on reaching a Post Office where my food parcel was, I loaded my pack with 14 days of food and basics and headed back into the wilderness and emerged 14 days later at another Post Office and parcel. Today, few do it traditionally, opting to carry 3 days of food and hike & hitch-hike out to a food store. Makes no sense physically and mentally, and makes the walk twice as long.

Sadly today sport is tainted with performance enhancing drugs. I have never taken any drug, only half a dozen aspirins over the years, and never seen a doctor. To excel there is one simple method. Be totally devoted and singleminded at your sport and whilst getting to peak performance realise that it is not just physical but having the correct mindset to do it.

I walk for it is the most natural and life enhancing activity you can do. Plus there is never any age limit; you can still walk when you are a hundred. So walk naturally one foot in front of the other and enjoy the landscape and before you know it you are at your destination, regardless of the mileage and mountains on the way. Glow with pride at making it on your own feet all the way and in an untainted way.

Revd. John N. Merrill - May 2017.

WALK THE NATIONAL FOREST WAY - 75 MILES

The author at the start.

In June 2017 I walked the National Forest Way from the National Monument Arboretum in Staffordshire to Beacon Hill in Charnwood Forest, Leicestershire.

It is a good walk through Staffordshire, South Derbyshire and in Leicestershire, following a mixture of paths and tracks. I camped where possible and Moira has both a Youth Hostel and campsite. You walk beside the Trent & Mersey Canal, through much woodland, past reservors and many historical buildings, including Calke Abbey. The final section is through Bradgate Park and onto the summit of Beacon Hill, a stunning climax. All in all an enjoyable 4 day walk in the Midlands.

www.nationalforestway.co.uk

Illustrated Talks
by Revd. John N. Merrill

John has countless talks on his recording breaking walks around the world.
For a full list contact John - Tel. 01992-762776
Email - marathonhiker@aol.com

His latest talks -

WALKING TO MONT ST. MICHEL - John has walked here twice - from Farnham via Winchester to Mont St. Michel (200 miles), and from Caen (100 miles) joining the annual pilgrimage walk organised by the Association of Chemins de Mont St. Michel. Both remarkable walks with the final 7km across the exposed sand, mud and rivers to the rock and abbey.

LONDON TO OXFORD PILGRIMAGE WALK - St. Frideswide Way - 93 miles. John discovers and traces the medieval pilgrimage route from Westminster Abbey to Christ Church Cathedral in Oxford, and the shrine of St. Frideswide. Then onto Binsey and her "forgotten" healing well; the Lourdes of the South.

WALKING ESSEX'S COASTLINE - 250 MILES - An exceptional walk around England's second largest county's coastline, rich in history, sea-birds and waders and more than 100 islands. A surprising journey.

WALKING MY WAY - The on going story of John's unique walking life, with some 219,000 miles walked. The stories and tales from his ground breaking walks around the world.

May the sun bring you new energy by day.
May the moon softly restore you by night.
May the rain wash away your worries.
May the breeze blow new strength into your being.
May you walk gbently through the world and
Know its beauty all the days of your life.

Apache blessing.

Look at the trees.
Look at the birds.
Look at the clouds.
Look at the stars ....
And if you have eyes
you will be able to see
that the whole of
existence is joyful.

Osho.

THE JOHN MERRILL MINISTRY
- a universal monk -
embracing & honouring
all faiths & none.

John has been following his own spiritual path all his life, and is guided. He was brought up as a Christian and confirmed at the age of 13. He then went to a Quaker Boarding School for five years and developed his love for the countryside and walking. He became fascinated with Tibet and whilst retaining his Christian roots, became immersed in Buddhism. For four years he studied at the Tara Buddhist Centre in Derbyshire. He progressed into Daoism and currently attends the Chinese Buddhist Temple (Pure Land Tradition) in London. With his thirst for knowledge and discovery he paid attention to other faiths and appreciated their values. Late in life he decided it was time to reveal his spiritual beliefs and practices and discovered the Interfaith Seminary.

'When the pupil is ready, the teacher will appear'. (Buddhist saying).

Here for two years he learnt in more depth the whole spectrum of faiths , including Jainism, Paganism, Mother Earth, Buddhism, Hinduism, Islam, Judaism, Sikhism, Celtic Worship and Shamanism. This is an ongoing exploration without end. He embraces all faiths, for all have a beauty of their own. All paths/faiths lead to one goal/truth. On July 17th. 2010 he was Ordained as a Multi-faith Minister.

'May you go in peace, with joy in your heart
and may the divine be always at your side.'

Using his knowledge and experience he combines many faiths into a simple, caring and devoted services, individually made for each specific occasion, with dignity and honour.
He conducts special Ceremonies -

Popular Funeral Celebrant and member of the Natural Death Society.

* Funerals * Memorial Services * Sermons * Weddings *Civil Partnerships
* Baby Blessings & Naming
* Rites of Passage * Healing Ceremonies * Pilgimages * Inspirational Talks
Qigong Teacher. Reiki Prationer.

For further information Contact John on -
Tel/Fax: 01992 - 762776 Mobile. 07910 889429
Email - marathonhiker@aol.com
Ministry site -www.thejohnmerrillministry.co.uk
All Faiths church - www.londoninterfaithchurch.co.uk

Revd. John N. Merrill, HonMUni
32, Holmesdale, Waltham Cross,
Hertfordshire EN8 8QY